Breakfast at TIMOTHY'S

Published by Lorimer Press
Printed in China

ISBN: 978-0-9897885-4-0
Library of Congress Control Number: 2014947825

Book Design by Leslie Rindoks
Photography, unless otherwise noted, © Kurt Rindoks

ADDITIONAL PHOTO CREDITS:
Tim & Yvette, pg xv; by Connie Gulley Duncan.
Biscuit Making Detail photos, pg 36; Behind the Scenes: photographer and
    stylists photos, pg 144 by Judy Latham.
Cow, pg 56; Flora, pg 59; Blackberries, pg 61; Sunrise, pg 77; Grapefruit,
    pg 88; Peaches, pg 90; Crabs, pg 133 by Yvette Harrold.
Bloody Mary, pg 119; After the Shoot, pp 160 by Meg Taylor.

Breakfast at TIMOTHY'S

RECIPES BY TIMOTHY O'LENIC, M.D.

LORIMER PRESS • DAVIDSON, NC

2015

DEDICATED TO YVETTE RENEE HARROLD,

MY ANCHOR TO THIS EARTH,

WHO ALLOWS ME TO SOAR THE ETHER OF CREATIVITY

EVER EXPERIMENTING IN THE GARDEN, OUR KITCHEN

AND IN MY SOUL

●

Table of Contents

WELCOME!

I've been working in a kitchen since age 14 when my friend Steve and I rode the bus to downtown Pittsburgh where we worked as porters at a private club. There, the Executive Chef gave me an informal apprenticeship, teaching me how to successfully navigate a professional kitchen. Since then, I have trained under and cooked with executive chefs from around the world — at a bakery, a delicatessen, a catering business and for a large hotel chain.

Somewhere along the line, I decided to pursue a medical career which took me out of professional kitchens. Today, I am a board certified anesthesiologist and critical care physician. My career choice has not diminished my passion for fine food, however, and I revel in the chance to share good food with my colleagues, friends and family.

My approach to cooking is eclectic, yet straight forward which makes it easy for you to jump right in and get busy in your kitchen! My mission is to help others develop a love for cooking and be able to share delicious food that nourishes our bodies and our souls.

As a doctor, I have a keen interest in helping others live as healthily as possible. It's true what they say, breakfast is the most important meal of your day, so why not make it as fun and tasty as possible?

Come on in and let's get started!

A FEW TIPS

INGREDIENTS

OIL

When I say olive oil, I mean extra virgin olive oil. I also like to use grapeseed oil for its clean, light taste and sunflower oil both for its taste and because it has a lower level of saturated fat.

SALT

When it comes to salt, texture, shape and mineral content affect its taste as well as how it interacts with other foods. There are times I call for kosher salt, often for its texture and the fact that tastes less salty than table salt. Kosher salt's large grains distribute easily and cling well to foods' surfaces. For some recipes, I prefer sea salt for its delicate, crunchy texture. (FYI, texture – not exotic provenance – is the main consideration. Look for sea salt with large, flaky crystals.)

SWEETENERS

I have fallen in love with agave syrup. It has 1.5 times the sweetening power per calorie compared to table sugar.

WATER

Filtering water can eliminate any odd tastes that may come from minerals inherent in tap water. You can use bottled water, but I'm trying to get away from contributing to all that plastic production.

PRODUCE

When shopping for fresh produce, the number one thing to consider is the season. Even though we are able to buy produce from around the world any time of the year – like tomatoes in the winter or strawberries in the fall – don't! Fruits and vegetables taste best when you buy them during their true growing season. Nature can enhance your cooking (and eating) when you allow it to bring you what it can in season.

Look for produce with vibrant colors and few, if any, soft spots. Check the stems; they should just be beginning to brown, not shriveled and grey. Fresh fruits and vegetables should be firm, full of life, and feel heavier than expected when you pick them up.

With a B.A. in chemistry, I know how important it is to avoid pesticides and other chemicals that artificially boost farmers' yields. On the other hand, as a physician, I see patients from all walks of life and realize that everyone cannot afford organic produce. So here is my advice:

1. Buy organic food as your budget permits. Nowadays, even large box retailers offer some organic options.
2. Shop at farmers' markets if possible. Support local farmers who work hard to bring you the best of what each season has to offer. Often, local growers will suggest new ways to enjoy what they have grown.
3. Consider planting your own garden. Yes, this is a reach for those of you who are convinced you don't have a green thumb. But I'll bet you know someone who does, so get their advice and give it a try!

UTENSILS & EQUIPMENT

The easiest way to thinly and uniformly slice vegetables is with a **mandolin**. Find a basic model; avoid those that look complicated. (I have one or two forgotten in a drawer that had too many bells and whistles.)

Buy a quality **blender**; you'll use it for more than smoothies and it should last for many years. (I really like my Vitamix.)

If you like to cook in larger quantities and freeze for future use, consider adding a **vacuum packer** to your kitchen. I have had a Magic Vac for more than a decade. Foodsaver makes a good model for home use; that's what I'd buy if I needed a new one. The vacuum removes the air, which contains water vapor that causes freezer burn. I generally don't find a need to double bag when I've vacuum packed food.

Let's talk about **non-stick pans**. When we think of non-stick pans, most of us envision Teflon. These are the pans I grew up with and used frequently in my own kitchen because of their non-stick properties and ease of cleaning.

Recently, Teflon has come under scrutiny due to concerns with the release of toxic compounds, mainly PFOA (perfluorooctanoic acid). As with many controversies, initially multiple media sources sound an alarm, then later the true facts emerge. To my knowledge, Teflon is safe to use as long as you follow a couple of rules:

1. Traditional non-stick pans should not be used for cooking with high heat (e.g., searing). This decreases the life of the pan, causes cracks on the surface, and can contribute to the release of toxic fluorine containing compounds.
2. Any non-stick pan that has cracks or visible damage to the surface should be thrown away and replaced.

I recently switched to ceramic non-stick pans. These pans cook evenly, are nonstick, thus allowing me to use less oil or butter, plus they are easy to clean. But remember, unlike heavy stainless steel pots and pans, non-stick pans do not last forever — a couple of years max before their performance declines and food begins to stick to the surface.

TECHNIQUES

MISE EN PLACE

Anyone who has ever worked in a professional kitchen knows that having everything ready before you begin is the most important step when cooking. In kitchen vernacular this is called *mise en place*. More specifically, this means reading the recipe at least twice (or until you have a feel of how things come together); gathering everything from the pantry and refrigerator; and ensuring you have the right cooking utensils at hand. If a recipe calls for chopped onions and peppers, chop them before you begin. If it calls for preheating the oven, turn it on at least 20 minutes before you start. I cannot emphasize the importance of this concept enough.

WARM YOUR PLATES

Use this little trick to keep food warm prior to serving. I use a warming drawer, but you can also heat your oven to 200° and warm plates there for 10-15 minutes.

TASTE AS YOU GO

Always sample your food while cooking. Does it need more salt and pepper? Is it too bland and in need of a sprinkling of herbs and spices? Or perhaps it needs a squeeze of fresh lemon? You be the judge, but never serve anything without sampling a little first.

SOMETIMES A LITTLE ACID HELPS

When you sample a dish and it tastes a little flat, try a squeeze of lemon juice, or a dash of quality vinegar. Chefs do this all the time and it makes a good meal, great! The acid in lemons, limes or vinegar adds a brightness to food, giving taste buds that "missing little something." This step is best done at the last moment, just before serving.

WORKING SAFELY

When working with meats, poultry and eggs, always wash your hands thoroughly to avoid exposure to salmonella. It is also important to use separate cutting boards and knives when preparing meats, eggs and vegetables. This will help decrease the risk of cross contamination.

LOW HEAT VERSUS HIGH HEAT

In general, I use high heat (medium high to high on most gas ranges) to sear meat, whether it be a piece of chicken, a firm fish fillet or a tender piece of beef. The concept is simple: High heat sears, or forms a browned crust on the surface, which adds a beautiful color to your food and adds flavor by caramelizing the inherent sugar in what you are cooking. Typically, when using this technique you will sear the side you will present to your guests, cooking about 70% of the total time. Then flip the meat, cooking to its desired doneness, usually about 30% of the total cooking time.

When not searing or browning meat, cooking on lower heat is best. For instance, eggs prefer to be cooked with low heat. Because eggs are protein dense, they become dry when cooked with high heat. Eggs turn out much creamier and softer when cooked slowly and gently with lower heat.

USING RESIDUAL HEAT

Food continues to cook after it is removed from the heat source. The food contains residual heat from the cooking process and this continues to heat and cook the food as it rests. Most chefs pull whatever they are cooking off the heat before it is completely done. (This includes pasta, meats and yes, eggs.) Remember this and you will never overcook anything again.

FREEZING BASICS

Even though I'm an advocate for using the freshest ingredients possible, there are times when you buy more than you need. This usually happens to me when I buy organic salmon. So, what I do is trim off what I need and then freeze the rest, often saving the extra for salmon cakes down the road. I highly recommend buying and using a vacuum sealer when freezing food.

Be sure to label every package that you put in the freezer. I usually use a sharpie marker to write the name and date on each bag. And remember to use your frozen goods within 6-8 weeks, 3 months at the absolute longest. Any longer than this in the freezer results in a loss of flavor.

FOR YOUR GENERAL WELL BEING

One the most healthy choices you can make is to eat at home. At home, you are in control – of the ingredients, and the portion size. After working in many restaurants, I can tell you they cut corners. It's nearly impossible for a restaurant to stock the very best ingredients. They often bolster the taste and texture of their food by adding fat,

salt and sugar. You'll know this if you've ever taken leftovers home, only to discover them later sitting in a ring of re-solidified butter or fat.

LOWER THE FAT, SUGAR & SALT

To lower the fat in any recipe, use a spray bottle filled with olive oil (or grapeseed oil) instead of the recommended butter. The flavor will be maintained and you will definitely save some calories. Also many of the new ceramic non-stick saute pans, (excellent for cooking eggs!) require little if any oil to keep things from sticking while cooking. This is an excellent and small investment to make when it comes to eliminating some unnecessary fat.

EAT YOUR FRUITS & VEGGIES

Nothing is better for you than fresh fruits and veggies. You don't have to go vegan or vegetarian, but you do have to eat your veggies. Vegetables contain the vitamins and fiber your body craves; they also help curtail hunger. When I start breakfast with a little fruit and lunch or dinner with a salad, my brain understands that I have started eating; fruits and vegetables are more filling than fats and sugars, and so my brain is better able to let me know when I've eaten enough.

DRINK PLENTY OF WATER

My seventh grade football coach used to say, "Flush out the toxins, drink more water." He was right. Water helps cleanse impurities from our bodies.

I recommend at least six, 8 oz. glasses per day. I start off with a glass before my morning shower and then continue to drink water all day long. I also keep some water on my nightstand.

ENJOY LIFE

One great way to get the most out of life is to relax and have fun. I recommend spending some time in your kitchen, cooking with, and for, those you love!

PORTION SIZE

Controlling portion size is another important step towards optimal health. A 6 oz. serving of meat and proteins (approximately the size of your palm) is the maximum serving size. I believe portion size is one of the main reasons restaurant dining has become such a fattening process. Not only do you not know how much butter, sugar and salt has gone into your meal, you are also being served a portion fit for at least two people not one.

USE SMALLER PLATES

Studies show that when food is served on smaller plates people tend to eat less. In cooking, presentation is half the battle; perhaps it is half the calories as well!

Eggs

Eggs are the cornerstone, the canvas, the heart of any breakfast menu, plus they are one of the world's most versatile and nutritious foods. An egg contains only 70 calories, yet packs a whopping six grams of protein and contains many of the essential vitamins and minerals our bodies crave.

Eggs are best when fresh. When you can, buy farm fresh eggs. Hens that exercise and eat grass and bugs produce eggs lower in cholesterol and saturated fat. Plus, their eggs are two times higher in the healthy omega-3s department. I usually buy mine Saturdays at the Davidson Farmers' Market. If you buy your eggs at a grocery store, always check the "use by" date. Eggshells are porous and therefore over time, eggs absorb air. A fresh egg will sink in a glass of water whereas an older egg will float. Another sign of a fresh egg is a plump, round yolk. As eggs age, the yolks absorb water from the white and the yolks become flat; the egg whites become thin and spread out more when cracked into the pan.

Poached Eggs

Poached eggs make for a healthy breakfast. They're also great on salads, sandwiches or pasta for lunch and dinner. There are a few tricks to poaching. First, you want to prevent, as much as possible, the egg white from spreading out, or feathering. Place a silicon cup (sold at many kitchen stores) in the water, or make a vortex in the water by swirling the water with a spoon prior to adding the egg. This takes a little practice so do the first few dozen or so over a sink! If you're cooking for a crowd, poached eggs can be cooled and reserved for several hours. Just reheat them in warm water prior to serving.

water
2 farm fresh eggs
1 t kosher salt
2 t white vinegar

Fill a large pot with water to a depth of about 1½ inches. Add the salt and vinegar and bring the water to a very quiet simmer over medium to medium-low heat. Crack each egg individually into a small ramekin. Stir the water with a large spoon to create a vortex in the center of the pot then add the first egg. Or, place a silicon cup in the heated water and slide the cracked egg into it. Once the white is set, repeat with the second egg. Cover the pan and turn off the heat. Cook for 6 minutes and then remove the eggs with a slotted spoon.

Serve poached eggs on toast or on English muffins. And for a delicious, healthy start to your day, add a little sauteed spinach and Swiss cheese.

Scrambled Eggs

Okay, maybe this is a little over the top as far as instructions are concerned, but I am on a mission to help you cook better so we're going to cover the basics.

RULE NUMBER ONE: Eggs love moisture.

RULE NUMBER TWO: Eggs appreciate a little TLC. A tender hand will render tender eggs, so scramble gently.

RULE NUMBER THREE: Don't overcook. Food continues to cook even after it's been removed from the heat. Take the eggs off the burner when they are just barely set, between runny and rubbery.

4 farm fresh eggs
2 T half and half*
1 T unsalted butter
salt and pepper, freshly ground and to taste

*You can also use whole milk, 2%, skim, or even water. For me, half and half works best.

Crack the eggs into a medium-sized bowl. Add the half and half and season with a little salt and pepper. Whisk the eggs until a slight amount of foam presents. I usually count to 21, my birthdate, but feel free to use your own number as long as it's in the double digits.

Heat a ten-inch, nonstick skillet over low heat. Give your pan enough time to thoroughly preheat, about 5 minutes. Add the butter and let it melt until the foaming subsides. Gently add the eggs and begin the slow process of moving them to and fro with a silicon spatula or wooden spoon. Move the eggs around deliberately, but gently, and continue to cook until they are just set. Soft, smooth, moist, glistening and fluffy is what you are looking for. Remember that the eggs will contain residual heat and will continue to cook when removed from the heat.

Yvette's Scrambled Eggs

USING FRESH HERBS

If you want to take your cooking to the next level, look no further than fresh herbs. Fresh herbs will bring your dishes alive with flavor and punch. Just a few precautions: Herbs with really strong flavors such as sage, rosemary and basil must be used judiciously (a little goes a long way). More neutral herbs like parsley, thyme and cilantro generally can be used with less discretion.

4 farm fresh eggs
1 T unsalted butter
2 T half and half
salt and pepper
1 T cream cheese, room temperature
½ t fresh basil, chopped
½ t fresh parsley, chopped
¼ t fresh chives, chopped

Crack the eggs into a medium-sized bowl. Add the half and half and season with a little salt and pepper. Now whisk the eggs until a slight amount of foam presents.

Heat a ten-inch nonstick skillet over low heat. Add the butter and let it melt until the foaming subsides. Gently add the eggs and move them to and fro with a silicon spatula or wooden spoon.

Remember the three rules for cooking perfect scrambled eggs: Moisture, TLC and Avoid Overcooking.

About half way through the cooking process, add the cream cheese (in small portions to allow it to spread out evenly) and the herbs. Stir this blend slowly and deliberately until the eggs are just set — not runny or rubbery — soft, smooth, moist and glistening. Serve with a few toasted pita crisps or a toasted baguette.

Mixed Mushroom Scramble *with Shaved Truffles*

French gourmand Jean Anthelme Brillat-Savarin called truffles "the diamond of the kitchen." Truffles (ectomycorrhizal fungi) are usually found near the roots of trees. Italian white truffles are very highly esteemed and are the most valuable on the market. In 2001, the *Tuber magnatum* truffles sold for between $1000–$2200 per pound. You can find more affordable truffles online, starting at around $22.50 per ounce.

2 T unsalted butter
½ C baby Portobello mushrooms, sliced thin
½ C chanterelle mushrooms, sliced thin
½ C shiitake mushrooms, stems removed, sliced thin
salt and pepper
2 t sherry
1 T unsalted butter
6 large eggs
3 T half and half
shaved white or black truffles to taste (optional, but incredible)

Melt the butter in a 12-inch non-stick saute pan over medium-low heat. Add the mushrooms, season with salt and pepper and saute until the water from the mushrooms has released and is mostly evaporated and they are slightly browned. Next, add the sherry and cook until it has absorbed, about 2-3 minutes. Remove from the heat and reserve.

Whisk the eggs with the half and half until light and airy. Melt the butter in a large non-stick pan and then add the eggs. Cook, stirring frequently, then season with salt and pepper. When the eggs are 80% done, add the reserved mushrooms and finish cooking until the eggs are just done and maybe just a little bit moist. Before serving, shave a little bit of truffle over top to really wow your taste buds. Enjoy!

Serves 2-3.

Southwestern Scrambled Eggs

I lived in Phoenix, Arizona for a couple of years and I still love to visit the area. I love the cacti, dry hot weather and the Ferraris innocently parked at the strip mall. (Yes, believe it!) One of my favorite activities when I'm in the Southwest, aside from eating, is hiking. You have to start early in the desert so before heading out I grab a protein bar. But once the hike is done, I head home for something more satisfying — like this egg dish.

4 farm fresh eggs
2 T half and half
salt and pepper
pinch of red pepper flakes
1 T unsalted butter
1 clove garlic, finely diced
2 T red onion, ¼" dice
1 small farm fresh tomato, diced (about a ½ C)
½ small jalapeno, seeded, ¼" dice (more if you like the heat)
½ fresh avocado, ½" dice
2 oz. Cotija cheese (or a mild feta)
1 T fresh cilantro, chopped

Whisk together the eggs, half and half, salt and pepper and red pepper flakes and set aside. Melt the butter in a 12-inch non-stick saute pan over low to medium-low heat. When the butter stops foaming add the onions and cook till they are soft and glistening, about 5 minutes. Then add the garlic and saute until softened, about 2-3 minutes more. Now add the egg mixture and cook slowly and gently.

Top with the chopped tomato, jalapeno, avocado slices, cheese and the cilantro.

You can also serve this as a breakfast burrito by spooning the cooked eggs on to a 6" tortilla. Add some hot sauce if you like!

Serves 2-3.

Fried Eggs *Sunny Side Up or Over Easy*

Practice makes perfect! When I was hired at a restaurant in Tampa, Florida, the chef asked if I would do the breakfast service for the first two weeks. The next thing I knew, I was in front of a large eight-burner stove with a gallon of melted butter and a case of eggs (24 eggs to a row, 12 rows deep). The chef said, Tim, why don't you practice flipping some eggs. I asked, How many, chef? All of them, he said. And I practiced flipping and flipping and flipping.

2 farm fresh eggs
1/2 T unsalted butter
salt and pepper

SUNNY SIDE UP

Start with a good, clean eight-inch, non-stick pan. (I'm really liking my new ceramic skillet's super smooth surface.) Place the pan over low to medium-low heat and melt ½ T unsalted butter. When the butter stops foaming add two eggs gently to the pan. Tilt the pan towards you when adding the eggs so they collect in a nice neat package. Season the eggs with salt and freshly ground pepper, then cover the pan. Keep covered for two minutes. Take a silicon spatula and run it around the outside of the eggs to loosen. Cook for another two or three minutes or until your desired doneness and then slide the eggs on to a warmed serving dish.

OVER EASY

Heat an eight-inch nonstick skillet over medium-low heat. Melt the butter and allow it to foam. When the foaming ceases crack the eggs gently into the pan. Tilt the skillet to keep the egg whites from running away from the yolks; a nice tight bundle is what you are going for. Nudging them with a wooden spoon also helps. Season the eggs with a little salt and freshly ground pepper and cook them slowly until the whites have set (mostly opaque, but not completely). Run a silicon spatula around the edges, loosening the eggs. Shake the skillet to make sure the eggs are mobile. Then raise the skillet and with quick wrist action, move the skillet away from you then toward you so the eggs flip. Cook for another minute and then gently slide onto a warmed plate to serve.

Jimi's Huevos Rancheros

This is probably the premier Tex-Mex egg breakfast and a favorite dish of mine. I learned how to cook the black beans from Jimi, one of my Cuban friends in Florida. He's a straightforward guy, just like this recipe.

Jimi usually uses dry beans and soaks them overnight. Here, to save time I've used canned beans. Use high quality canned beans (like the Goya brand) for the best results and rinse the beans thoroughly before using. Remember they are already cooked, so when reheating and seasoning the beans, keep your cooking time to a minimum, otherwise the beans will be soft and mushy.

1 15 oz. can black beans, rinsed
2 T olive oil
½ yellow onion, ¼" dice
¼ red bell pepper, ¼" dice
1 small clove garlic, chopped fine
½ t ground cumin
½ t chili powder
½ C chicken broth
1 T fresh cilantro, chopped
4 flour tortillas
8 large eggs
2 T unsalted butter, divided
½ C Cotija cheese
1 jalapeno, sliced (optional)
your favorite hot sauce
salsa (see page 84)

Warm four plates in a 250° oven.

Rinse the beans well and reserve. Saute the onion, bell pepper and then the garlic until glistening, but not browned. Add the spices and the chicken broth, bring heat to medium high and reduce the broth by half. Reduce heat to low or simmer, then add the beans, toss to mix well and cook for about 5 more minutes to allow all the flavors to marry. Remove from the heat.

Wrap the tortillas in moist paper towels and warm in the preheated oven for 5 minutes, or 10-12 seconds in the microwave.

Meanwhile, heat the butter (½ T, for each two eggs) over medium-low heat and cook until desired doneness. Remember a good clean non-stick pan is required here. If you like the top of the eggs cooked all the way through, cover the pan with a plate to seal in the heat.

Place a heated tortilla on each warmed plate, top with 3-4 T of the bean mixture, 2 cooked eggs, a sprinkle of fresh cilantro and 2 T Cotija cheese (or queso fresco). Add salsa (page 84), sliced jalapeno and hot sauce to complete.

Serves 4.

Soft Boiled Eggs

The perfect soft boiled eggs have silky whites and gooey, soft centers that call for the simple pairing of buttery toast. Best results occur when you bring eggs to room temperature before boiling.

2 farm fresh eggs
water
salt and pepper

In a medium pot add the eggs and fill with cold water so that about one inch of water surrounding the eggs and they are able to float. Turn the heat to high and bring to a boil. Once the water begins to boil, cover the pot and remove it from the heat. Let eggs sit undisturbed 3-6 minutes, depending on the doneness you want. Place them, round end up, in two egg cups, crack the top part of the shell with a knife and serve in the shell.

Hard Boiled Eggs

Home-made hard boiled eggs taste so much better than mass-produced version generally served in cafeterias and salad bars. And they're so easy to do it's silly to settle for less. Consider boiling your eggs on Sunday night and then you can enjoy them throughout the week.

6 farm fresh eggs
water

In a medium pot add the eggs and fill with cold water so that about one inch of water surrounding the eggs and they are able to float. Turn the heat to high and bring to a boil. Once the water begins to boil, cover the pot and remove it from the heat. Let eggs sit undisturbed for 10 minutes and then remove to an ice bath to stop the cooking.

Shirred Eggs *with Prosciutto and Fontina Cheese*

Shirred eggs, sometimes called baked eggs, sometimes called eggs *en cocotte,* depending on the exact cooking style, are certainly a throw back recipe. Shirred eggs are soft, flavorful and luxurious.

4, 6-inch ramekins
2 T unsalted butter, divided
2 thin slices prosciutto, cut in half
8 farm fresh eggs
4 t heavy cream
4 T Fontina cheese, grated
salt and freshly ground pepper
12 parsley leaves

Preheat oven to 375°.

Grease each ramekin with about ½ T unsalted butter. Place one piece of prosciutto to cover the bottom and along the sides a bit. Crack two eggs into each ramekin, add 1 t cream to each and season with salt and pepper.

Place the ramekins on a baking sheet and place in the preheated oven. Bake for 10 minutes and then remove from the heat. Now sprinkle the eggs with the Fontina cheese and bake an additional 10-15 minutes or until they are done to your liking. Garnish each ramekin with three parsley leaves.

Serves 4.

Shirred Eggs *with Tomatoes & Herbes de Provence Crouton*

Herbes de Provence, dried herbs characteristic of traditional southern French cooking, include savory, marjoram, rosemary, thyme, oregano. And though it is not commonly used in traditional southern French cooking, in the U.S., *Herbes de Provence* mixtures also contain lavender.

4, 6-inch ramekins
2 T unsalted butter
6-8 tomato slices, ½" thick
4 slices French bread, ¼" thick
olive oil
2 t Herbes de Provence
8 farm fresh eggs
4 t heavy cream
salt and pepper
4 t Parmesan cheese, grated

Preheat oven to 375°.

Grease each ramekin with ½ T butter and then place a layer of tomato slices in the bottom. Place the ramekins on a baking sheet and bake for 7-10 minutes, until the tomatoes start to become soft. Remove from the oven.

While the tomato is cooking, brush each slice of bread with a little olive oil and toast. You can use a medium-sized skillet over medium heat to do this. When they are toasted, sprinkle each slice with about ½ t *Herbes de Provence*.

Now place a toast slice in each ramekin and then crack two eggs into each. Add 1 t cream to each and season with salt and pepper. Place the tray into the oven and bake for 5-7 minutes, or until the white just starts to set. Now remove the tray from the oven, sprinkle each ramekin with Parmesan cheese and then bake for an additional 7-10 minutes or until desired doneness. Garnish with a little more *Herbes de Provence* and serve immediately.

Serves 4.

Shirred Eggs *with Swiss Chard & Emmental Cheese*

My first experience with shirred eggs was at a small breakfast spot in Charleston, South Carolina. When I returned home, I went on a dramatic search for the perfect shirred egg vessel so I could duplicate the dish in my kitchen. This recipe is my take on that delicious experience. Hopefully, I'm doing them justice.

4, 6-inch ramekins

2 T unsalted butter, room temperature

1 T olive oil

½ yellow onion, ¼" dice

10 leaves Swiss chard, large stem removed, and chopped

8 eggs

4 t heavy cream, whole milk or whatever dairy product you have in the fridge!

½ C Emmental cheese, grated

1 t fresh rosemary, chopped

Preheat oven to 375º. Grease four 6" ramekins with ½ T butter each.

Heat a 12-inch saute pan over medium heat, add the olive oil and saute the onion until soft and glistening. Now add the Swiss chard and cook until all the water is released from the chard. Divide the Swiss chard and onion mixture into each of the casserole dishes and crack 2 eggs into each of these. Add 1 t of cream or milk and season with salt and pepper. Now sprinkle the cheese and rosemary on top.

Place ramekins on a baking sheet and bake for 20 minutes or until the eggs are firm and finished. Serve in the ramekins. Be careful, they will be hot!

Serves 4.

Toad in a Basket

This recipe is a great way to get some protein into your little ones in the morning. It is a favorite of my young friend Dylan, a baseball fanatic and possible future star.

I use Challah bread because I love its sweet and eggy flavor, but you can use any bread you like. There are just two rules: First, make sure to slice the bread at least 1-inch thick; and second, make sure the slice is large enough to allow a good margin of bread all around the "hole." Be creative; try different cookie cutters...have fun!

4, 1-inch thick slices Challah bread
3 T unsalted butter. melted
4 large eggs
salt and pepper

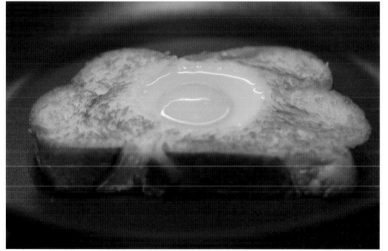

Preheat a large skillet over medium-low heat.

Using a 2-inch biscuit cutter (or cutter of your choice), cut a hole in the center of the bread, making sure to keep the hole surrounded by bread and crust. Brush a little melted butter on both sides of the Challah and then place 2-4 slices into the hot skillet. Work in batches of two if necessary; do not over crowd. Cook the bread until golden brown on one side, then flip it over to brown the other side.

Crack an egg into each of the "holes" and cover the skillet and cook until the egg is just cooked through and the bottom of the bread is browned. Season with a little salt and pepper and serve immediately.

Serves 2-4.

Classic French Omelette

The classic French omelette is golden and soft, never browned and is slightly runny or underdone. If this is not to your liking you can always cook the eggs a little longer. No worries here friends, just don't make the mistake I did and serve "over cooked" eggs to a classically trained French chef!

1 T unsalted butter
3 large eggs, whisked well
1 T half and half
2-3 turns salt and freshly ground pepper
2 T shredded Gruyere cheese
½ t fresh thyme, chopped fine

Warm serving plate in 200° oven.

Preheat an eight-inch, non-stick pan over medium-low heat.

Melt the butter in preheated pan. Allow butter to sizzle a bit and make sure to coat the sides of the pan. (Remember eggs prefer to be cooked on lower heat so don't be afraid to adjust the temperature down, slow is good here.) Combine the whisked eggs with the half and half, and season with salt and pepper. Using a silicon spatula, move the cooked eggs from the edges of the pan to the center and do this about four times (north, south, east and west). Turn off the heat.

Add the cheese and fresh thyme to the middle of the circle. Now fold the omelette in thirds. Fold the first third so that it covers the cheese and herbs, fold the second third on top of the first. Cook the omelette for 1-2 more minutes and then slide the omelette off the pan onto the preheated plate.

If you like your eggs a little more well done, cook until the bottom of the omelette is set and the top still a little wiggly. Loosen the sides from the pan with your spatula and then with a swift motion, move the pan forward then backward to flip the omelette. You can add the omelette fillings at this point then just fold the omelette in half to serve.

Caprese Style Omelette

Caprese salad is made with garden grown tomatoes, fresh buffalo mozzarella, just picked basil, and is served with a drizzle of extra virgin olive oil and aged balsamic vinegar. Italians enjoy this delicious salad in the summer when tomatoes are at their peak.

Burrata cheese is fresh mozzarella on steroids. Burrata means "buttered" in Italian. It's that rich. It is fresh mozzarella with a creamy center, fresh cheese at its best, and its creaminess makes this omelette extremely silky.

1 T unsalted butter

3 eggs

1 T half and half

4 cherry tomatoes, chopped

2 thin slices of burrata cheese (or fresh buffalo mozzarella cheese)

1 T fresh basil, chopped

Warm serving plates in 200° oven.

Preheat an eight-inch, non-stick pan over medium-low heat.

Melt the butter in the preheated pan. Allow the butter to sizzle a bit and make sure to coat the sides of the pan. Whisk the eggs with the half and half, season with salt and pepper and add to the pan. Using a silicon spatula, move the cooked eggs from the edges of the pan to the center. Do this about four times (north, south, east and west). Turn off the heat. Add the tomatoes, cheese and basil. Fold in half to serve.

For a more well done omelette, cook until the eggs are nearly set, yet still a little wiggly, loosen the sides from the pan with your spatula and then with a swift motion, move the pan forward, then backward to flip. Add the tomatoes, cheese and basil. Fold in half to serve.

(A small drizzle of a fragrant olive oil over the top just before serving sends this omelette over the top!)

Egg White Omelette *with Asparagus & Feta*

When I travel to Torrey Pines, near San Diego, California (an amazing part of the country), I enjoy walking on the beach and admiring the beautiful cliffs. I also enjoy an egg white omelette at one of my favorite hotels there. One bite of this omelette and I am transported to Torrey Pines State Park.

4 egg whites
2 T half and half
salt and freshly ground pepper
2 T unsalted butter, divided
2 asparagus spears, chopped into 1" pieces
4 cherry tomatoes, quartered
1 T mild feta cheese, crumbled
6-8 fresh oregano leaves
salt and freshly ground pepper (white pepper is a nice touch!)

Warm serving plates in 200° oven and preheat a ten-inch, non-stick pan over medium-low heat.

Make sure to chop, slice and dice everything you need for this recipe first before you start! (*Mise en Place!*)

Whisk the egg whites and the half and half until thoroughly combined and a bit frothy. Season with salt and pepper.

Melt 1 T butter over medium heat. Saute the tomatoes and asparagus pieces until the asparagus turns a beautiful light green (about 4 minutes), remove from the pan and reserve. Now adjust the heat to medium low and add 1 more T of butter and allow to it melt. Next, add the egg whites.

Using a silicon spatula, move the eggs from the edges of the pan to the center and do this about four times (north, south, east and west). Cook until the eggs are nearly set, yet still a little wiggly. Loosen from the sides of pan with your spatula and then with a swift motion, move the pan forward, then backward to flip. Cook for a little longer. Add the asparagus, tomatoes and feta cheese then fold in half.

Slide the omelette onto a pre-warmed plate and sprinkle with a few oregano leaves. Makes 1 large or 2 small servings.

Bryan's Beach Boy Omelette

Bryan, my nephew, lives in San Diego and as most Californians do, he loves avocados. This is his favorite "Cali-style" omelette.

I use a mandolin to get super thin slices of the red onion — it is certainly one of my must haves in the pantry! If you don't have a mandoline yet, buy the basic model, the simpler, the better. (I have several expensive devices that I still have not figured out.)

2 egg whites
1 whole egg
1 T half and half
salt and freshly ground pepper
½ T unsalted butter
4 thin slices of avocado
red onion, sliced super thin (about 3 slices)
2 T micro greens, mixed herbs or arugula

Warm serving plates in 200° oven and preheat a ten-inch, non-stick pan over medium-low heat.

Gently whisk the egg, egg whites and the half and half together. Season with salt and pepper.

Over medium-low heat melt the butter in a non-stick pan until it stops foaming. Add the eggs and cook them slowly, moving the wet ingredients, north, south, east and west until they are mostly cooked through. Now, flip the omelette (yes you can!) and add the avocado slices, the red onion and the micro greens to the center, spreading evenly.

Fold the omelette in half and slide onto a prewarmed plate.

Carolina Blonde & Green Omelette

Dedicated to all my
North Carolina friends.

It's hard for me to believe that I've lived in North Carolina for more than 14 years!

If you live in, or visit, the South, include Asheville (one of my favorite mountain towns) in your plans. It is funky and hip with great restaurants, amazing hiking and biking trails, plus the Biltmore Estate. I like to begin a day in Asheville with a Carolina Blonde and Green Omelette. This makes my heart sing and readies me for a hike in the Pisgah National Forest.

2 egg whites
1 whole egg
1 T half and half
salt and freshly ground pepper
½ T unsalted butter
2 T white cheddar, grated
2 slices maple black pepper bacon (see page 105)
1 T fresh green onion, sliced thin, include a bit of the green part
1 t fresh parsley, chopped

Warm serving plates in 200° oven and preheat a ten-inch, non-stick pan over medium-low heat.

Gently whisk the egg whites with the whole egg and the half and half. Season with salt and pepper.

Melt the butter over medium-low heat until it stops foaming. Add the eggs and begin to cook them gently, moving them from the edge of the pan to the center, north, south, east and west. When the eggs are mostly firm, but not cooked through, flip.

Add two slices of cooked maple black pepper bacon, the cheddar cheese and the green onion. Fold the omelette in half, garnish with the parsley and serve.

Crispy Pancetta Omelette

Pancetta, Italian bacon, is made from pork belly. It is sold raw, and must be cooked before eating. Pancetta is cured and *unsmoked*, while bacon in the US is cured and smoked. It is sometimes sold sliced paper thin, or cubed.

3 farm fresh eggs
1 T half and half
3 thin slices of pancetta
¼ C red bell pepper, ¼" dice
1 shallot, ¼" dice
2 T unsalted butter, divided
1 t fresh parsley, chopped

Warm serving plates in 200° oven and preheat a ten-inch, non-stick pan over medium-low heat.

Whisk together eggs and half and half and set aside.

Saute the pancetta over medium heat until crispy. Remove to a chopping board and chop fine.

Melt 1 T butter and saute the red pepper until soft and glistening. Then add the shallot and cook for another 2-3 minutes. Remove from the heat and add to the chopping board with the pancetta.

Now, turn the heat to low, melt the other T of butter in the saute pan and start to cook the eggs, moving them from the edge of the

pan to the center, north, south, east and west. When the eggs are mostly firm, but not cooked through, flip. Add the pancetta and shallots. Fold the omelette in half and slide onto a prewarmed plate. Garnish with parsley.

Frittata *with Mushroom, Leek & Fontina*

Frittatas are eggs, cheese, meat, veggies combined — Italian style. Perfect, but not fussy. They can be served hot, straight from the oven or later in the day, at room temperature for a light snack.

The sky is the limit with the ingredients, just remember to cook any raw meat or veggies before adding them to the eggs.

1 T olive oil

1 T unsalted butter

1 leek, chopped white and a small amount of green as well

4 oz. crimini mushrooms

8 eggs

¼ C creme fraiche

1 T fresh parsley, chopped

1 t fresh thyme, chopped

½ C Fontina, shredded

salt and pepper to taste

Preheat oven to 350°.

In a ten-inch, non-stick, oven-proof saute pan, melt the butter into the olive oil, over medium heat.

Add the mushrooms and cook until all liquid is absorbed (about 10 minutes). Add the leeks and cook until slightly browned. Reduce heat to low.

In a large bowl whisk together eggs, creme fraiche and the herbs. Pour the egg mixture into the pan and then top with the cheese. Cook until the sides are set (about 5 minutes) and then transfer the pan to the oven. Cook for 20-30 minutes or until the center is almost set and still slightly wiggly. The edges of the frittata should be turning golden brown. (Remember eggs continue to cook after they are removed from the heat.)

Serves 6-8.

Asparagus & Gruyere Frittata

Gruyere, a hard yellow cheese, is named after the town of Gruyeres, Switzerland. It is sweet but slightly salty, with a flavor that varies widely with age – creamy and nutty when young, and more assertive, earthy and complex when aged. When fully aged (five months to a year) it tends to have small cracks which add a slightly grainy texture. I love using Gruyere because it adds a savory quality without overshadowing other ingredients; plus, it's an excellent melting cheese.

2 T olive oil
2 T unsalted butter
¼ C yellow onion, ¼" dice
8 asparagus spears, chopped into ½" pieces
8 eggs, whisked
¾ C Gruyere, shredded
¼ C Parmesan cheese, grated
1 T fresh parsley, chopped
salt and pepper to taste

Preheat oven to 400°.

Heat an eight-inch, oven-proof, non-stick pan over medium heat and melt the butter into the olive oil. Saute the onions and asparagus until the onions are glistening and the asparagus is bright green. Remove the asparagus and set aside.

Meanwhile whisk the eggs, cheeses and parsley and season with salt and pepper. Add this mixture to the hot pan and cook until the bottom is set (about 3-4 minutes), moving the sides of the frittata towards the middle with a silicon spatula. I like to place about 6-8 asparagus spears in a pinwheel pattern on the top just before baking.

Now place the pan in the oven and bake until the eggs are just cooked through about 10-12 minutes. Allow the frittata to cool and then cut into wedges. Serve hot, or later at room temperature. Serves 4-6.

Frittata *with Caramelized Onions & Roasted Peppers*

This frittata requires two additional techniques: caramelizing onions and roasting bell peppers. (See pages 82-83.) I usually make more than I need since the process is a little time consuming. Once you master these techniques, you can use caramelized onions and roasted bell peppers for French onion soup, topping pizzas or as a great addition to pasta dishes. They will stay nicely refrigerated for about a week.

1 T unsalted butter

2 T olive oil

¼ C roasted red peppers (about ½ pepper)

½ C caramelized onions (about one onion)

2 t fresh rosemary, chopped

12 farm fresh eggs, whisked

½ C Pecorino Romano

salt and freshly ground pepper

Preheat oven to 400°.

Caramelize onions (see page 82) and roast peppers (see page 83).

In a 12-inch, non-stick saute pan melt the butter and oil together over low heat. Now remove the pan from the heat and start to arrange the veggies. Arrange the pepper slices in a pinwheel pattern, spacing evenly. Add the onions and distribute evenly over the surface. Now whisk the eggs with the rosemary, cheese and salt and pepper. Carefully add this mixture to the pan so as not to wreck your beautiful design.

Place the pan back on the stove over medium-low heat and cook until the bottom is set. Then place the pan in the oven and bake until the eggs are almost cooked through, about 10 minutes. Allow the frittata to cool a bit and cut into wedges. Serve warm or at room temperature. Serves 6-8.

Mushroom, Fontina & Herb Quiche

Quiche should be a part of everyone's cooking repertoire. Like the frittata, there are endless combinations of ingredients. My only suggestion is don't overdo the filling; allow the eggs and cream to work their magic. Furthermore, a quiche can be made ahead of time (perfect for parties!) and can be served warm or at room temperature.

Because quiche requires a crust, let me be the first to admit that I am not the best of bakers. So when I am craving baked goods that require crust, I use Pillsbury brand crust for a real home-made look. Mrs. Smith's frozen deep dish crust works well, too.

1 9-inch pie crust
1 egg white, beaten lightly
3 T unsalted butter, divided
2 medium shallot, chopped ¼"
2 C baby Portobello mushrooms, sliced 1/8" thick
2 large eggs, plus 2 egg yolks
½ C whole milk
¾ C half and half, room temperature
⅓ C fresh parsley, chopped
2 pinches of salt
Freshly ground pepper to taste
¼ t fresh ground nutmeg
1 C Fontina cheese, grated

Preheat oven to 375º.

Roll the pie crust into a nine-inch pie dish. (If using a premade frozen crust, do not thaw first.) Pick the bottom of the crust with a fork several times. Cover the edges of the dough with foil and bake for about 10-12 minutes. Remove the foil and brush the pie crust edges with the egg white. Allow to cool.

While the crust is baking, heat a 12-inch saute pan over medium heat. Melt 1 T of the butter then add the shallots and cook them until they are translucent (about 4 minutes). Remove to a separate plate. Now melt the other 2 T of butter and saute the mushroom slices until they are golden brown and have released all their juices.

Lightly beat the milk, half and half, eggs, parsley, salt pepper and nutmeg in a medium bowl. Add the cooked mushrooms and shallots to the bottom of the pie crust and then slowly pour the egg mixture over, keeping the mushrooms and shallots evenly distributed. Bake the quiche for 25 minutes, or until the center is almost set and puffy. You may have to cover the edges of the crust with foil half way through the baking process so it does not burn. Cool the quiche for 30 minutes and then serve by cutting into wedges.

Serves 6-8.

Bacon, Gruyere & Thyme Quiche

Here's my take on the French classic, Quiche Lorraine. This quiche contains bacon (or ham), eggs, Gruyere and sometimes a pinch of nutmeg. I like to add fresh thyme to this dish for a fresh herbal surprise that I think really makes a difference.

1 9-inch pie crust

1 egg white, beaten lightly

6 slices center cut bacon, cooked crisp then chopped

2 eggs

2 egg yolks

¾ C half and half, room temperature

1 C grated Gruyere cheese

1 t fresh thyme, chopped

pinch of nutmeg

salt and pepper

Preheat oven to 375º.

Prick the bottom of the crust several times with a fork. (If using a premade frozen crust, do not thaw first.) Cover the edges of the crust with aluminum foil and then bake until a light brown, about 10-12 minutes. Remove the foil and brush the pie crust edges with the egg white. Allow to cool.

Saute the bacon until crisp, remove to cool and then chop into bite-sized pieces.

Whisk the eggs until foamy. Add the milk, then whisk to combine.

Add the egg and milk mixture to the precooked crust and season with salt and pepper. Then sprinkle in the bacon, cheese and thyme, distributing them evenly. Bake in the preheated oven for 25 minutes or until the center is puffy, but still moves a bit like Jello. (You may need to cover the edges with foil halfway through.) Remember custards will continue to cook after they are removed from the heat. Allow the quiche to cool and then cut into 6-8 wedges.

Serves 6-8.

Feta, Spinach & Artichoke Quiche

The classic combination of feta and spinach is perfect for salads and egg dishes like this quiche. The addition of a small amount of garlic and prepared artichoke hearts give this dish a slight pungency that does not overwhelm the palate, but adds significantly to the flavor and texture. I think you'll love this flavor combination.

1, 9-inch pie crust
1 egg white, beaten lightly
4 C fresh spinach, large stems removed
1 clove garlic, minced
2 T olive oil
6 oz. jar of artichoke hearts, chopped
2 whole eggs
2 egg yolks
¾ C half and half, room temperature
salt and pepper
½ C feta cheese, crumbled (and more for garnish)

Preheat oven to 375°.

Prick the bottom of the crust several times with a fork. (If using a premade frozen crust, do not thaw first.) Cover the edges of the crust with aluminum foil and then bake until a light brown, about 10-12 minutes. Remove the foil and brush the pie crust edges with the egg white. Allow to cool.

Heat a large, non-stick saute pan over medium heat. Add the oil and once it comes to temperature, add the spinach leaves. Cook the leaves, tossing often with tongs. Add the garlic and artichokes hearts and cook until the spinach is softened and most of its moisture has evaporated. Remove this to a colander and allow any excess water to drain.

Meanwhile, whisk the eggs, yolks, half and half until combined and season with salt and pepper. In the prebaked pie crust, add the reserved spinach mixture evenly over the bottom. Now carefully add the egg mixture. Sprinkle the feta cheese evenly on top. Place in the preheated oven and cook until the egg is set, but still jiggly. Do not overcook. Remove from the oven and allow to cool. Cut into 6-8 wedges when you are ready to serve.

Summer Zucchini & Basil Quiche

Zucchini is such a versatile vegetable! From pan fried, to grilled with a little olive oil, sauteed with onions and peppers, to zucchini blossoms stuffed with ricotta cheese, what's not to love? Another great way to use zucchini is in this quiche.

1, 9-inch pie crust

1-2 zucchini, sliced into rounds about ¼" thick (about 1 C)

1 T unsalted butter

1 small yellow onion, ¼" dice (about 1 C)

1 T olive oil

1 egg white, beaten lightly

2 eggs

2 egg yolks

¾ C half and half, room temperature

¼ C Parmesan cheese

salt and freshly ground pepper

6-8 fresh basil leaves

Preheat oven to 375°.

Prick the bottom of the crust several times with a fork. (If using a premade frozen crust, do not thaw first.) Cover the edges of the crust with aluminum foil and then bake until a light brown, about 10-12 minutes. Remove the foil and brush the pie crust edges with the egg white. Allow to cool.

Season the zucchini slices with salt and pepper and saute in the butter over medium-low heat until slightly browned on both sides. Remove to a clean plate to cool. Next saute the onions in the olive oil until soft and glistening, about 6-7 minutes. Remove those to a clean plate as well to cool.

Whisk together the eggs and half and half, season with salt and pepper.

Add the zucchini slices to the bottom of the crust in a circular fashion, one layer thick. Distribute the cooked onions on top of the zucchini and then add the egg mixture. Next place the basil leaves in a circular pattern and submerge them just a little bit under the egg mixture and sprinkle with the parmesan cheese. Season with salt and pepper. Bake the quiche (on a baking sheet to prevent a mess) for 25 minutes or until the center is puffy and set, but still slightly moist. Allow the quiche to cool and then slice into 6-8 slices.

Grains

Grains, one of the five major food groups, help provide the building blocks for a healthy diet. Women need 5- to 6-ounce equivalents daily, while men need 6- to 8-ounce equivalents, depending on age. (1-ounce equivalent equals one slice of bread, 1 cup of ready-to-eat cereal or ½ cup of cooked rice, pasta or cereal.) Try to make half of your grains whole grains which contain the entire grain kernel — the bran, germ and endosperm.

I use a variety of grains in my kitchen, from rolled oats, flax and chia seeds, to oat and wheat bran. And yes, I use good old-fashioned, all purpose flour as well.

The more complicated recipes I reserve for special occasions like holidays or when family and friends visit. They are delicious, serve a small crowd easily and can be made ahead so that I can spend more time with my guests and less time in the kitchen.

I hope you'll branch out and try a few of these, especially the ones that you might not be familiar with.

Basic Biscuits

After living in the South for many years, I have come to thoroughly enjoy great, flaky biscuits. When out of town guests (especially those from up North) visit, I treat them to some real home-made biscuits.

Here's the secret: COLD. Yep, chill *everything*. I even stash the flour in the freezer for a few minutes, and wash my hands in cold water before handling the dough.

2 C all purpose flour
1 T baking powder
¼ t baking soda
1 t salt
5 T unsalted butter, cold *
1 C buttermilk (or whole milk)

* place butter in the freezer for 10-15 minutes before using

Preheat oven to 450°.

Mix the dry ingredients together in a food processor. Cut the butter into small pieces and try to keep it cold — VERY COLD. Add the butter to the dry ingredients and pulse briefly. The key to making biscuits is to keep the butter cold and make a chunky dough...keep this combination lumpy, not uniform.

Add the milk, and pulse just a few more times to bring together.

Place the dough on a lightly floured, cold surface. Wash your hands with cold water and then knead gently for one minute. Gently shape the dough into a ¾-1" thick circle and cut into 2" rounds with a biscuit cutter.

Place the biscuits (almost touching) on a parchment-lined baking sheet. Baste with a little melted butter. Bake for 15 or so minutes, until golden brown.

Makes 6-8 biscuits.

Biscuits *with Rosemary Ham & Gruyere*

Of course there are an endless number of ingredients you can combine to make a breakfast sandwich. Here the classic ham and cheese biscuit is elevated by the taste and scent of fresh rosemary. Adding a small spoon of whole seed mustard or raspberry jam takes this small package over the top. Ask your deli to cut the rosemary ham (I prefer Boar's Head) in ⅓" slices.

4 freshly baked biscuits (see page 37)
4 slices rosemary ham, sliced thin
8 T Gruyere cheese, grated
½ t fresh rosemary, chopped fine

Heat a large skillet over medium-low heat. Add the ham slices and cook until warmed. Flip the ham and top each piece with 2 T of grated cheese and then sprinkle each with a pinch of the fresh rosemary. Cover the skillet and heat until the cheese melts.

Meanwhile, slice the biscuits in half and place them on a warmed serving plate. When the cheese has melted, slide one piece of ham onto each split biscuit, cover with the top and gently press to allow the melted cheese and the top of the biscuit to become one.

A little dollop of grainy mustard or raspberry jam is a nice touch, and a slice of fresh melon makes for the perfect accompaniment.

Biscuits & Gravy

If calories didn't count, I'd eat biscuits at least once a week. Unfortunately, calories do add up, so I reserve this delicious breakfast for special occasions.

A note on using sage: Sage is a wonderful herb and is probably under-utilized by us cooks. The only thing to remember is that sage is very powerful...less is always best.

4 freshly baked biscuits (see page 37)
1 lb breakfast sausage, crumbled
1-2 sage leaves, sliced super thin
4 T unsalted butter
4 T all purpose flour
2 C whole milk, room temperature
pinch of red pepper flakes (optional)
salt and freshly ground pepper

Heat a large skillet over medium-high heat. Add the crumbled sausage and cook through, stirring often. Remove to a separate plate but leave the rendered fat in the skillet. Reduce heat to medium and add the butter. Once the butter has stopped foaming, add the flour 1 T at a time and stir continuously. (Yes, you are making a blonde roux.) Allow the roux to thicken and turn a lovely, light tan color. Keep stirring — now is not the time to leave the stove for any reason. Add the milk slowly and continue to stir with a whisk, breaking up lumps as they occur. Allow to thicken. If you were patient with your roux, and I know you were, you will be reveling in the silky texture that is happening in your pan right now!

Add the reserved sausage and stir to blend. Finally, add the fresh sage and red pepper flakes. Season with salt and pepper and allow all these rich flavors to release.

Split each biscuit in half and cover with about ¼ C of the sausage gravy. (I like to serve this with a couple of eggs cooked over easy. Just slide them right on top of the gravy.)

Sausage, Egg & Brie Biscuit

I've lightened up this classic recipe a bit so you can enjoy it like spa food...well almost.

Brie, the soft cows' milk cheese, is named after the French province where it originated. Some folks wonder if the outer, grayish hard rind should be removed prior to eating. Don't! The rind is meant to be eaten, and adds to the flavor and character of the cheese.

2 poached eggs (see page 2)
2 home-made biscuits
2 chicken sausage patties (see page 106)
2 T Brie cheese, divided
2 pinches fresh rosemary, chopped

Preheat oven to 200°.

Poach the eggs as described on page 2. Place in an oven-proof bowl or ramekin and slip these into the preheated oven to keep warm.

Heat an eight-inch, non-stick pan over medium heat. Add the chicken sausage and cook until browned on both sides. Turn off the heat and add the cheese on top of the sausage and cover the pan with a plate. When the cheese has melted, about 1-2 minutes, uncover the pan.

Slice biscuits in half, place the sausage and melted cheese on the bottom. Top with the poached egg. Sprinkle with fresh rosemary and enjoy.

Zesty Cranberry Scones

2 C all purpose flour

⅓ C turbinado sugar (sugar in the raw)

1 T baking powder

½ t Kosher salt

1 T lemon zest (about 1 lemon)

8 T unsalted butter, (freeze for 5 minutes)

½ C dried cranberries (toss first in a small
      amount of flour)

1 large egg

¾ C cream

½ t vanilla extract

EGG WASH:

1 egg

1 T water

Scones are traditionally connected with Scotland, Ireland and England, but no one knows for sure where they originated. One claim, probably not the best, but certainly the most lofty, says that scones were named for the Stone (scone) of Destiny, a stone upon which Scottish kings once sat when they were crowned.

Regardless of where they originated, scones belong in your cooking repertoire. They are very easy to make and also quite delicious.

Preheat oven to 375°.

Place the first 4 ingredients together in a large mixing bowl. Add the lemon zest and blend together at the lowest speed with the paddle attachment. Now remove the butter from the freezer and cut into 1 T size pieces. Add butter pieces to dry ingredients and mix on low until butter pieces are the size of small marbles, about 1 minute. Dough should be lumpy and not uniform. Add the cranberries and mix for 30 seconds more.

Whisk together the egg, cream and vanilla extract. Add this slowly to the dry ingredients and mix at the lowest setting until the dough just comes together (about 1-2 minutes). Lumpy and wet is what we are looking for.

Place the dough on a floured surface and work it briefly, shaping into a ¾- to 1-inch thick circle. Using a dough cutter or knife, cut in half and then cut each half into 4-5 wedges. Whisk egg and water together briefly and brush over dough. Sprinkle with a little sugar.

Place the wedges about 1 inch apart on a parchment-lined baking sheet. Bake for 18-22 minutes or until golden. Let rest for 15 minutes, then enjoy. Makes 8-10 scones. (Scones are best the first day but will keep for at least two.)

Almond Scones

You may have heard two different pronunciations for "scone." Which is authentic? They both are! The word is pronounced "skahn" (rhymes with gone) in Scotland and Northern England, and pronounced "skoan" (rhymes with own) in the south of England, which is also the pronunciation most commonly heard in the US and Canada.

2 C all purpose flour
1/3 C turbinado sugar (sugar in the raw)
1 T baking powder
½ t Kosher salt
½ C sliced almonds
8 T unsalted butter (freeze for 5 minutes)
1/2 t almond extract
1 large egg
¾ C cream

EGG WASH:
1 egg
1 T water

Preheat oven to 375°.

Place the first five ingredients in a large mixing bowl. Blend together at the lowest speed with the paddle attachment. Now remove the butter from the freezer and cut into 1 T size pieces. Add butter pieces to dry ingredients and mix on low until butter pieces are the size of small marbles, about 1 minute. Dough should be lumpy and not uniform. Add the almonds and mix for 30 seconds more.

Whisk together the egg, cream and almond extract. Now add this slowly to the dry ingredients and mix at the lowest setting until the dough just comes together (about 1-2 minutes). Lumpy and wet is what we are looking for.

Place the dough on a floured surface and work it briefly, shaping into a ¾- to 1-inch thick circle. Using a dough cutter or knife, cut in half and then cut each half into 4-5 wedges. Whisk egg and water together briefly and brush over dough. Sprinkle with a little sugar and salt. Place the wedges about 1 inch apart on a parchment-lined baking sheet. Bake for 18-22 minutes or until golden. Let rest for 15 minutes, then enjoy. Makes 8-10 scones. (Scones are best the first day but will keep for at least two.)

Apricot & Orange Scones

In the UK, plain or currant scones are traditionally served with afternoon tea. Plain scones are spread with jam or lemon curd, then topped with a dollop of clotted cream. This is known as cream tea or Devonshire tea.

In the US, where afternoon tea is a rare event, scones are considered more of a breakfast/brunch bread alternative. Varieties such as these with fruit are considered "fancy" scones and require no toppings.

2 C all purpose flour
1/3 C brown sugar
1 T baking powder
½ t Kosher salt
½ C dried apricots, diced
1 T orange zest
8 T unsalted butter (freeze for 5 minutes)
1 large egg
1 T heavy cream
¾ C sour cream
1/2 t vanilla extract
1 T freshly squeezed orange juice

EGG WASH:
1 egg
1 T water

Preheat oven to 375°.

Place the first 6 ingredients in a large mixing bowl. Blend together at the lowest speed with the paddle attachment. Now remove the butter from the freezer and cut into 1 T size pieces. Add butter pieces to dry ingredients and mix on low until butter pieces are the size of small marbles, about 1 minute. Dough should be lumpy and not uniform.

Whisk together the egg, cream, sour cream and vanilla extract. Now add this slowly to the dry ingredients and mix at the lowest setting until the dough just comes together (about 1-2 minutes). Lumpy and wet is what we are looking for.

Place the dough on a floured surface and work it briefly, shaping into a ¾- to 1-inch thick circle. Using a dough cutter or knife, cut in half and then cut each half into 4-5 wedges. Whisk egg and water together briefly and brush over dough. Sprinkle with a little sugar. Place the wedges about 1 inch apart on a parchment-lined baking sheet. Bake for 18-22 minutes or until golden. Let rest for 15 minutes, then enjoy. Makes 8-10 scones. (Scones are best the first day but will keep for at least two.)

Meyer Lemon & Poppy Seed Scones

A cross between a lemon and a mandarin orange, the Meyer lemon has smooth golden skin the color of a fresh egg yolk. It also has a thin edible rind, a high volume of juice and lacks the tartness of a traditional lemon. Meyers may be substituted for regular lemons whenever you want a burst of lemon flavor without the acidic bite.

COOL TRIVIA: The Meyer lemon was a lowly houseplant in China until the US Department of Agriculture sent Frank N. Meyer, an agricultural explorer (yes, that was his actual job title!) to China In the early 1900s to collect new plant species.

2 C all purpose flour
1/3 C turbinado sugar (sugar in the raw)
1 T baking powder
½ t Kosher salt
2 T poppy seeds
zest of one Meyer lemon (about 1 T)
8 T unsalted butter (freeze for 5 minutes)
1 large egg
¾ C cream
1 T freshly squeezed Meyer lemon juice

EGG WASH:
1 egg
1 T water

Preheat oven to 375°.

Place the first 6 ingredients in a large mixing bow. Blend together at the lowest speed with the paddle attachment. Now remove the butter from the freezer and cut into 1 T size pieces. Add butter pieces to dry ingredients and mix on low until butter pieces are the size of small marbles, about 1 minute. Dough should be lumpy and not uniform.

Whisk together the egg, cream and lemon juice. Add this slowly to the dry ingredients and mix at the lowest setting until the dough just comes together (about 1-2 minutes). Lumpy and wet is what we are looking for.

Place the dough on a floured surface and work it briefly, shaping into a ¾- to 1-inch thick circle. Using a dough cutter or knife, cut in half and then cut each half into 4 wedges. Whisk egg and water together briefly and brush over dough. Sprinkle with a little sugar and salt. Place the wedges about 1 inch apart on a parchment-lined baking sheet. Bake for 20 minutes or until golden. Let rest for 15 minutes, then enjoy. Makes 8 scones. (Scones are best the first day but will keep for at least two.)

Anytime Cornbread

"*The North thinks it knows how to make corn bread, but this is a gross superstition. Perhaps no bread in the world is quite as good as Southern corn bread, and perhaps no bread in the world is quite as bad as the Northern imitation of it.*"

—Mark Twain
(Samuel Langhorne Clemens, 1835-1910)

Cornbread has been called a "cornerstone" of Southern US cuisine. This cornbread is so good you can serve it with pride anytime of the day.

1 T bacon fat

1 C stone ground yellow cornmeal

½ C all purpose flour

½ C bread flour

1 t baking powder

½ t baking soda

¾ t salt

1 T light brown sugar

1 C whole milk

2 eggs, beaten lightly

2 T unsalted butter, melt and cool

1 C roasted fresh corn, cut from the cob

Preheat oven to 425°, then preheat a nine-inch, cast iron skillet for about 20 minutes in the preheated oven.

Sift the dry ingredients together in a medium-sized bowl. Add the remaining ingredients (milk, eggs, butter and corn) into another bowl and whisk to combine. Add half of the wet ingredients to the dry ingredients and mix gently. Then add the remaining wet to dry and mix again gently. Lumpy is good here, do not over mix!

Melt the bacon fat in the preheated cast iron pan, then add the cornbread mix. Transfer to the oven and bake for about 20 minutes or until the top is golden brown and a toothpick placed into the center comes out clean. Let the bread cool before cutting. Makes 8 servings.

Jalapeno Cornbread

The jalapeno is a medium-sized chili pepper. Compared to other chilis, the jalapeno heat level varies from mild to hot depending on cultivation and preparation. The heat is concentrated in the membrane surrounding the seeds.

I highly recommend that you use latex gloves when you handle these babies. Cutting, skinning or seeding fresh jalapenos can cause skin irritation. Do not let your hands come in contact with your eyes, as this can cause painful burning and redness.

1 T bacon fat

1 C stone ground yellow cornmeal

½ C all purpose flour

½ C bread flour

1 t baking powder

½ t baking soda

¾ t salt

1 T light brown sugar

1 C whole milk

2 eggs, beaten lightly

2 T unsalted butter, melt and cool

1 C roasted fresh corn, cut from the cob

1-2 seeded, minced, jalapenos

Preheat oven to 425°, then preheat a 9-inch, cast iron skillet for about 20 minutes in the preheated oven.

Sift the dry ingredients together in a medium-sized bowl. Add the remaining ingredients (milk, eggs, butter and corn) into another bowl and whisk to combine. Add half of the wet ingredients to the dry ingredients and mix gently. Then add the remaining wet to dry and mix again gently. Add jalapenos during last mixing. Lumpy is good here, do not over mix!

Melt the bacon fat in the preheated cast iron pan, then add the cornbread mix. Transfer to the oven and bake for about 20 minutes or until the top is golden brown and a toothpick placed into the center comes out clean. Let the bread cool before cutting. Makes 8 servings.

Yve's Zucchini Bread

If you have ever grown your own zucchini you know that as the summer progresses your zucchini plants really begin to produce fruit — sometimes so much that you need a variety of different ways to prepare and eat all those lovely things.

This bread is my go to recipe for just these times. The bread is slightly sweet but still somewhat savory. I like to serve it with just a little soft unsalted butter. (This bread also freezes well.)

1 C pecan pieces, toasted
3 C all purpose flour
1 t fine sea salt
2 t cinnamon
1 t freshly ground nutmeg (use a micro-plane)
1 t baking soda
1 t baking powder
2 C light brown sugar

1 C sunflower or other vegetable oil
3 eggs, lightly beaten
2 C grated zucchini
zest of 1 lemon
1 t lemon juice
cooking spray

Preheat oven to 350°.

In a saute pan, toast the pecan pieces over medium heat until lightly toasted (about 3-4 minutes).

Sift the flour, salt, baking soda and baking powder together and then add the sugar and spices and mix together thoroughly. Now mix together the wet ingredients in a separate bowl.

Grate the zucchini into the wet ingredients and blend well.

Combine wet ingredients and dry ingredients thoroughly.

Coat 8" x 4" loaf pans with cooking spray and then pour in the batter. Bake the bread in the preheated oven for about 50-55 minutes or until a toothpick inserted in the middle comes out clean. Serve with warmed butter and your favorite jam.

Makes 2 loaves.

Mom's Eastern European Nut Rolls

My mom only served these nut rolls on special occasions, specifically Christmas and New Years. Some of my fondest childhood memories include enjoying these on Christmas Eve. Mom served them slightly toasted with a little fresh butter.

You will crave them all year long.

¼ C warm water (105°)

¾ C whole milk

3 T granulated sugar

1 package active yeast

1 t salt

1 egg, beaten

1 t vanilla extract

4 T melted unsalted butter, slightly cooled

3 C all purpose flour, sifted

1½ t baking powder

FILLING

8 oz. walnuts, chopped fine

½ C granulated sugar

1 T melted, unsalted butter

2 T evaporated milk

2 T whole milk

¼ t vanilla extract

pinch of salt

Warm water and milk to 105-110°. Place the water and milk into a bowl for a standing mixer then add the sugar and yeast and allow the yeast to bloom. It should double in size. Now add the salt, beaten egg, vanilla and 4 T of melted butter and mix to combine. In a separate mixing bowl sift the flour and baking powder together. Add flour mixture, a little at a time, mixing on your lowest setting for 2 minutes. Turn the mixer to low-medium setting and mix the dough until it forms a ball and begins to separate from the sides.

Remove dough from the mixer and divide in half. Place one piece of dough on a well floured surface and roll into a 9"x12" rectangle. Repeat with the remaining piece of dough.

For the filling, pulse the walnuts to a fine grind using a food processor. Combine remaining ingredients and mix together well. To assemble, spread filling in a thin layer over rolled out dough, leaving a 1" border on all sides. (You may have a little extra left over filling.) Now roll the dough from the long edge, making a long and skinny log. Fold ends under to seal. Repeat with remaining dough. Place rolls on a well buttered sheet pan and cover with plastic wrap. Refrigerate overnight. In the morning, preheat oven to 350°. Remove plastic wrap and bake rolls until golden brown, about 35-40 minutes. Allow to cool and then slice into ½" pieces to serve.

My Classic Granola

Granola, a mixture of nuts, oats, dried fruits and grains, is a great breakfast food. My only word of advice with granola is limit your serving size to one quarter cup. Though good for you, granola can be high in fat and calories due to the nuts and dried fruit. I usually pair a couple of tablespoons of granola with low fat yogurt for breakfast. If you buy granola from the store instead of making it at home, try to avoid those with high fructose corn syrup, one of those sneaky, calorie-laden ingredients that manufacturers like to add.

cooking spray
¼ C canola or vegetable oil
3 C rolled oats
½ C wheat germ
1 C slivered almonds
½ C pecans, chopped
¼ t salt
½ C brown sugar
2 T flax seed
2 T maple syrup
2 T honey

Preheat oven to 300°.

Coat a baking sheet with a thin layer of cooking spray.

Mix everything but the syrup and honey together in a large bowl. Then slowly add the syrup, then the honey, distributing both evenly. Mix until everything is thoroughly combined. Spread in as thin a layer as possible on the prepared baking sheet. Bake for 30-40 minutes, turning the mixture every 15 minutes to get an even bake. Remove from the oven and allow to cool.

Store in an airtight container. Granola will stay fresh for about a month.

Super Antioxidant Granola

This granola is packed full of antioxidants, the Michael Jordans of the food world. Antioxidants minimize cell damage that may lead to things you want to avoid like heart disease, cancer and Alzheimer's.

Nuts, one of the most balanced foods on the planet, offer a good dose of "healthy" fats. Red berries, like cranberries, contain ellagic acid that may help protect against cancer-causing agents. And blueberries contain many of the vitamins and minerals known to strengthen the immune system and help lower inflammation.

cooking spray
1 C pecans
½ C sliced almonds
½ C sliced cashews
3 C rolled oats
¼ C maple syrup
¼ C dark brown sugar
2 T whole brown flax seeds
2 T chia seeds
2 T honey
¼ C grapeseed oil
½ t Kosher salt
½ C dried cranberries
½ C dried blueberries

Preheat oven to 300°.

Coat a baking sheet with a thin layer of cooking spray or oil.

Roast the nuts in a preheated oven for 5-8 minutes. Make sure to use unsalted nuts! Otherwise, the granola may turn out too salty. Let the nuts brown slightly, do not overcook. Now place the oats and nuts into a large mixing bowl. Working slowly, add the maple syrup in a couple of swirls and using a wooden spoon or silicon spatula, stir to combine. Add the dark brown sugar, flax seed, honey, canola oil and salt and again stir to combine. Now place the mixture in a single layer onto a large, prepared baking sheet.

Bake at 300° for 30-40 minutes, stirring every 15 minutes until the granola becomes crispy. Remove from the oven and allow the granola to cool. Break up the granola and then add the dried fruit.

Store in an airtight container or a glass jar. Granola will stay fresh for about a month.

NOTE: I also spray my measuring cups with a little oil to keep the sugar and syrup from sticking.

Timothy's Hawaiian Granola

There is no place on earth quite like Hawaii. The endless coastline, lush forests imbued with fragrant tropical flowers, impressive active volcanoes and the abundance of seafood, fresh fruits and nuts.

This recipe combines some classic Hawaiian flavors. When eaten on a warm day, with a mild breeze, this can transport me to the Islands.

Is that a whale I see?

cooking spray
4 C rolled oats
1 C macadamia nuts, halved
½ C sliced almonds
½ C chopped pecans
¾ C shredded sweet coconut
¼ C dark brown sugar
¼ C maple syrup
2 T honey
¼ C canola oil
¼ t fine sea salt
¼ C dried pineapple, ¼" dice
¼ C dried apricot, ¼" dice
¼ C dried mangos, ¼" dice

Preheat oven to 300°.

Coat a baking sheet with a thin layer of cooking spray or oil.

Combine the oats, nuts and coconut in a large mixing bowl. Set aside.

Combine the sugar, syrup, honey, oil and salt in a 12-inch sauce pan. Over medium-low heat allow the sugar to dissolve and the items to combine.

Add the sugar mixture to the dry ingredients (do not add the fruit just yet) and bake in a thin layer on a prepared baking sheet for about 30-40 minutes, turning the mixture every 15 minutes or so to get an even bake. Remove from the oven and allow to cool.

Break the granola into chunky pieces and add the dried fruit. Store in a large glass container; it will last about a month.

Aloha!

California Dreamin' Granola

One of my frequent daydreams is how and when I will manage to move to California! Since my first trip there as a child I have been enamored with everything the state has to offer. It is also where I was first introduced to home-made granola. I immediately realized the significant difference in taste from store bought. This is my ode to those California dreams!

cooking spray
3 C rolled oats
½ C sliced almonds
½ C sunflower seeds, roasted and salted
½ C pecan pieces
2 T flax seed
1 T orange zest
½ t salt
¼ t ground cardamom
½ C brown sugar
¼ C grapeseed oil
2 t vanilla extract
4 T unsalted butter, melted

Preheat oven to 300°.

Coat a baking sheet with a thin layer of cooking spray.

Mix the next nine ingredients together in a large bowl. Then add the grapeseed oil and vanilla extract and mix thoroughly.

In a medium sauce pan, melt the butter over medium heat and add to the bowl. Mix well.

Place the mixture in a thin layer on the prepared baking sheet. Bake for 30-40 minutes, stirring about every 15 minutes to get an even bake. Remove from the oven and allow to cool. Store in a large glass container; it will last about a month.

Muesli

This old-fashioned Swiss cereal mix can be eaten plain, or with yogurt.

To enjoy it as the Swiss do, soak a bowlful in milk overnight. After this long milkbath, the oats and wheat bran become soft and luxurious.

4½ C rolled oats
½ C wheat bran
½ C oat bran
½ C wheat germ, toasted
1 t fine sea salt
½ C raisins
½ C dried cranberries
½ C slivered almonds
½ C hazelnuts
1 T flax seeds
¼ C dark brown sugar (optional)

Combine the rolled oats, wheat bran, oat bran and wheat germ with the salt and mix thoroughly. Add the dried fruit a couple of pieces at a time so that no big lumps form. Add the nuts and flax seeds (and brown sugar if using) and mix again.

This Muesli can be stored in an airtight glass jar for about a month.

If you want to be authentic, combine ½ C of the Muesli with 1 C 2% milk and allow it to sit overnight. Top with a few fresh berries and it will be ready to gobble up in the morning.

Oatmeal

Here are a few simple facts: 1. Old-fashioned (rolled) oats taste much better than instant oats; and 2. The extra few minutes it takes to cook the real deal pays you real dividends.

A half-cup serving of either instant or rolled oats contains the same amount of carbs and protein, and each weighs in at 150 calories. Both also contain 4 grams of fiber, which helps block the absorption of cholesterol. But rolled oats have a lower glycemic index, which means they provide better sustained energy. (Instant oatmeal often has added ingredients such as caramel color and guar gum that you may wish to avoid.)

2 C water
¼ t salt
1 C rolled oats
1 T honey
1 T unsalted butter

In a small sauce pan, bring the water and salt to a boil. Add the oats, turn the heat to very low and cover the pan. Stir once or twice or until the water is absorbed. Add the honey and the butter and mix together. Allow the oatmeal to rest for 5 minutes. Makes two servings.

See how easy this is? Now, take a look at some seasonal varieties.

Winter Oatmeal

2 C water
¼ t salt
1 C rolled oats
1 T honey
1 T unsalted butter
2 T C golden raisins
2 T dried figs, chopped into bite-sized pieces
2 T maple syrup

If you look at the ingredients on a canister of rolled oats, you will usually see only one ingredient...rolled oats. Hard to find a healthier choice for a nice, hot breakfast on a frosty morning.

In a small sauce pan, bring the water and salt to a boil. Add the oats, turn the heat to very low and cover the pan. Stir once or twice or until the water is absorbed. Add the honey and the butter and mix together. Allow the oatmeal to rest for 5 minutes.

Add the raisins, figs and syrup. Makes two servings.

Spring Oatmeal

Once the world begins thawing out, we tend to think more about working out. (Beach trips and bathing suits are not that far away.) If your morning routine includes an ab workout, your overall metabolism needs to be working top notch for that exercise to really pay off. Guess what? What you eat for breakfast plays a huge role in how well your metabolism works. Eating oatmeal may be the secret to powering your workout and boosting your metabolism.

¼ C blueberries
¼ C blackberries
¼ C strawberries
pinch of salt
1 T sugar
2 C water
¼ t salt
1 C rolled oats
1 T honey
1 T unsalted butter

Clean and rinse the berries and place them in a medium mixing bowl. Add the salt and sugar and allow the berries to macerate for about an hour.

In a small sauce pan, bring the water and salt to a boil. Add the oats, turn the heat to very low and cover the pan. Stir once or twice or until the water is absorbed. Add the honey and the butter and mix together. Allow the oatmeal to rest for 5 minutes, then serve.

Add the berries to the oatmeal when you are ready to serve. Makes two servings.

Summer Oatmeal

With all the incredible fruit available in the summer it is hard to choose. My best strategy for summer oatmeal is to use fruits that are fresh, ripe and perhaps a little eccentric!

2 C water

¼ t salt

1 C rolled oats

1 T honey

1 T unsalted butter

¼ C fresh mango, diced

¼ C fresh banana, diced

2 T coconut flakes

2 T agave syrup

In a small sauce pan, bring the water and salt to a boil. Add the oats, turn the heat to very low and cover the pan. Stir once or twice or until the water is absorbed. Add the honey and the butter and mix together. Allow the oatmeal to rest for 5 minutes.

Mix the amazing fresh fruits together, add to the oatmeal and enjoy! Makes two servings.

Fall Oatmeal

Need another reason to dig in to a bowl of oatmeal? Oats are rich in omega-3 fatty acids, which can lower blood pressure and triglyceride levels. There's also good evidence that diets high in omega-3 fatty acids help stave off rheumatoid arthritis. Oats also contain folate, a key nutrient in heart health, and potassium, also good for your heart and kidneys.

2 C water
¼ t salt
1 C rolled oats
2 T honey
1 T unsalted butter
⅛ t ground cinnamon
⅛ t ground cardamom
⅛ t ground nutmeg
zest of ½ an orange
¼ C dried apples, chopped

In a small sauce pan, bring the water and salt to a boil. Add the oats, turn the heat to very low and cover the pan. Stir once or twice or until the water is absorbed.

Stir in the honey, butter and spices. Then add the orange zest and dried apples. Allow the oatmeal to rest for 5 minutes. Makes two servings.

64

Blackberry & Creme Fraiche French Toast

French toast was one of my favorite treats for breakfast as a kid, and it still is! Blackberries are another one of my favorites. This recipe combines both.

Blackberries grow everywhere it seems and picking a few of these black beauties for breakfast just seems right. I remember many times picking berries with my brothers and sister and bringing them home to Mom who used them to make a blackberry pie. *Heaven!*

4 fresh eggs
½ C whole milk
1 T agave syrup or honey
4 slices white bread, 1" thick
3 T unsalted butter, divided
1 C fresh blackberries
1 T sugar
1 C creme fraiche
pure maple syrup (optional)

Whisk the eggs, milk and honey in a medium-sized bowl until a little foamy.

Soak the bread slices about 30 seconds per side in the egg mixture. Do one piece at a time, right before you are ready to cook. If you soak the bread prematurely it will become too soggy and will fall apart when you cook it.

Melt the 1 T butter in a 12-inch, non-stick pan over medium heat. Add the blackberries and sugar and cook until the berries begin to burst (about 3-4 minutes), remove from heat.

Heat the remaining 2 T butter in a non-stick saute pan and add the slices of bread. Cook until golden brown on both sides and then spoon the berry mixture over the top. Finish with a dollop of creme fraiche.

French Toast *with Fresh Peaches, Blackberry Jam & Mint*

French toast, also known as eggy bread or gypsy toast, is very easy to prepare. I have just two recommendations: Please use bread that is at least 1" thick, and do not soak the bread for too long in the egg mixture or it will fall apart when it is being cooked.

So remember: *Soak and cook, soak and cook.*

4 pieces white bread, 1" thick (like Texas bread)
3 farm fresh eggs
¾ C whole milk
1 t quality pure vanilla extract
1 t ground cinnamon
3 T unsalted butter, divided
3 fresh peaches, skin removed, ½" slices
8 mint leaves, sliced super thin
4 T blackberry jam
4 small mint sprigs, for garnish
pure maple syrup, to taste

Whisk the eggs in a medium-sized bowl until a little foamy. Add the milk and vanilla extract and whisk to combine. Now here comes the tricky part. Add the cinnamon a little at a time and whisk to incorporate. If you add the cinnamon all at once it will cling to itself and not distribute evenly.

Soak the bread slices about 30 seconds per side in the egg mixture. Do one piece at a time right before you are ready to cook.

Heat a 12-inch, non-stick saute pan on medium heat, and melt half of the butter. Once the bubbling ceases, add four pieces of bread (if they fit well) or two pieces of soaked bread into the pan. Cook one side until it turns golden brown, about 3-4 minutes. Flip and repeat on the other side. Then plate to serve.

Add 1 T of the blackberry jam onto the center of each piece of French toast and spread it out a little bit. Top with the fresh peach slices and the fresh mint leaves. Serve with warmed maple syrup (boysenberry syrup goes well with this, too!). Enjoy. Serves 2-4.

Bananas Foster French Toast

Here is a fun and sweet recipe, inspired by the original Bananas Foster at Brennan's in New Orleans.

In New Orleans, as well as France and Belgium, French toast is called *pain perdu*, i.e., "lost" or stale bread. Cooks reclaimed the stale or "lost" bread by dipping it in a mixture of milk and eggs to soften it and then fried it in butter.

4 fresh eggs
½ C whole milk
½ t cinnamon
1 t vanilla
pinch of sea salt
4 slices Challah (or another egg bread), cut 1" thick
4 T unsalted butter, divided
2 ripe bananas, sliced into ½" discs
¼ C dark rum
¼ C dark brown sugar
2 T filtered water
½ C chopped walnuts

Whisk the eggs, milk, cinnamon and salt. Place the Challah bread slices in the egg mixture and coat both sides well (about 30 seconds per side).

Meanwhile, in a 12-inch saute pan, melt 2 T of the butter and cook the banana slices over medium heat until they are slightly golden. Remove them from the heat and place them on a clean plate.

Pour the rum, brown sugar and water into the same saute pan and return to medium heat. Simmer, allowing the sugar to dissolve completely and reduce the rum/water mixture by half. Add the reserved bananas, cook until warmed through and reserve.

Using a non-stick saute pan melt the remaining butter and saute the Challah French toast until golden brown (about 3-4 minutes per side).

Serve the toasts individually, spooning the banana and rum reduction on, and sprinkle with the chopped walnuts. Serves 2-4.

Croissant French Toast

Here is a *doubly* French recipe!

My first experience with French toast made with croissants was in a busy restaurant in Indianapolis. I was blown away. I'm not sure if this recipe holds a candle to theirs but I think it's at least a close second.

4 croissants, cut in half lengthwise
3 large eggs
¾ C half and half
1 t pure vanilla extract
½ t ground cinnamon
⅛ t ground nutmeg
4 T pecan pieces
pure maple syrup
2 T unsalted butter, divided

In a large mixing bowl whip the eggs until slightly foamy then add the half and half and slowly add the spices, making sure to blend together well.

Melt 1 T unsalted butter in a non-stick skillet over medium heat.

Place two split croissants into the egg mixture and allow them to soak for about 30 seconds per side. Place the croissants into the preheated pan and cook until golden brown on both sides. Remove to a preheated plate, sprinkle with pecan pieces and top with a little maple syrup. (If you are cooking for a crowd, the croissants can be kept warm on a baking sheet in a 200° oven.) These go great with some crisp bacon and fresh berries! Serves 2-4.

Classic Pancakes

Pancakes have been around for millenia! The ancient Greeks enjoyed theirs (called 'kreion') drizzled with honey. An old Roman cookbook by Apicius includes what may be the first ever recorded recipe for pancakes. Even George Washington loved pancakes for breakfast. (Historians report that he thoroughly drowned his in maple syrup.)

Here is my basic recipe for pancakes...probably easier to follow than old Apicius's.

2 C all purpose flour

1 T baking powder

½ t salt

1½ T sugar

2 C whole milk

2 eggs

2 T butter, melted, but not hot

1 t vanilla extract

Preheat griddle.

Sift all the dry ingredients and mix together. Whisk the eggs until they become frothy then mix in all the other wet ingredients. Add the dry ingredients to the wet in small amounts and stir gently. Do not over mix; lumps are perfectly fine, even encouraged. Over mixing will cause the pancakes to be tough, and we want light and fluffy!

Melt a little extra butter (about 1-2 T depending on how many you are cooking at once) on the griddle and then ladle a ¼ C of the pancake batter onto the griddle, keeping plenty of space between each. Cook about 3-4 minutes until you see bubbles form on the outside. Flip and cook another 1-2 minutes, or until golden brown, and serve. Makes 6-8 pancakes.

If you're serving a crowd, this recipe can be doubled and pancakes can be kept warm in an 200° oven.

Blueberry Maple Pancakes

A few fun facts pertaining to this dish:

- January 28th is National Blueberry Pancake Day.

- Thank the Algonquins for discovering maple syrup. They collected sap from Canadian sugar maple trees and boiled it (much the same way we process maple syrup today) and then enjoyed it as a beverage.

2 C all purpose flour
1 T baking powder
½ t salt
1½ T sugar
2 C whole milk
2 eggs
2 T butter, melted, but not hot
1 t vanilla extract
1 C fresh blueberries
2 T unsalted butter
½ C pure maple syrup

Preheat griddle.

Sift all the dry ingredients and mix together. Whisk the eggs until they become frothy then mix in all the other wet ingredients. Add the dry ingredients to the wet in small amounts and stir gently. Do not over mix; lumps are perfectly fine.

Melt a little extra butter on the griddle and then ladle the batter by ¼ cupfuls onto the griddle, keeping plenty of space between. Cook about 3-4 minutes until you see bubbles form on the outside. Flip and cook another 1-2 minutes, or until golden brown, and serve.

Melt the butter in a small sauce pan then add the blueberries. Cook until the blueberries begin to burst. Add the maple syrup and then remove from the heat. Top the pancakes with this mixture. Makes 6-8 pancakes.

Peach & Toasted Pecan Pancakes

I encourage you to try a little sorghum with these pancakes. Before the advent of daily vitamins, doctors prescribed sorghum as an effective supplement for patients suffering from low iron, calcium and potassium.

Sorghum replaced sugar cane as a major crop in the South in the late 1800s. With the decrease in available farm labor during WWII, however, sorghum gave way to glucose-based syrups. Today, sorghum is enjoying a bit of a comeback. Very versatile, it can be substituted cup for cup in any recipe that calls for molasses, honey, corn syrup or maple syrup.

1 C pecan pieces, toasted

2 C all purpose flour

1 T baking powder

½ t salt

1½ T sugar

2 C whole milk

2 eggs

2 T butter, melted, but not hot

1 t vanilla extract

1 T unsalted butter

3 fresh peaches, skinned and sliced, ½" thick

½ C sorghum syrup (or maple syrup)

Preheat the oven to 400°. Place the pecan pieces in an oven-proof pan and toast them until golden brown (about 6 minutes).

Preheat griddle. Sift all the dry ingredients and mix together. Whisk the eggs until they become frothy then mix in all the other wet ingredients. Add the dry ingredients to the wet in small amounts and stir gently. Do not over mix; lumps are perfectly fine.

Melt a little extra butter on the griddle and then ladle the batter by ¼ cupfuls onto the griddle, keeping plenty of space between. Cook about 3-4 minutes until you see bubbles form on the outside. Flip and cook another 1-2 minutes, or until golden brown, and serve.

Meanwhile, melt the butter in a saute pan then add the peaches. Cook until they are softened and warm (about 3 minutes). Add the sorghum syrup to the peaches and then spoon this over the pancakes. Sprinkle with the toasted pecans and serve. Makes 6-8 pancakes.

Strawberry Banana Mascarpone Pancakes

There's something special about banana pancakes. Jack Johnson wrote a song about them and that album (*In Between Dreams*) went double platinum.

These pancakes are triply special as they combine bananas with strawberries and mascarpone.

Mascarpone, an Italian cheese from Lombardy, is a thick, double or triple cream, cream that is on its way to becoming butter.

2 C all purpose flour

1 T baking powder

½ t salt

1½ T sugar

2 C whole milk

2 eggs

2 T butter, melted, but not hot

1 t vanilla extract

1 pint fresh strawberries, rinsed and quartered

1 banana, peeled and sliced, 1/4" rounds

1 t lemon zest

1 C mascarpone cheese

Preheat griddle. Sift all the dry ingredients and mix together. Whisk the eggs until they become frothy then mix in all the other wet ingredients. Add the dry ingredients to the wet in small amounts and stir gently. Do not over mix; lumps are perfectly fine.

Gently mix the strawberries, bananas, lemon zest and the mascarpone cheese in a small mixing bowl. Set bowl aside in a warm place while you make the pancakes.

Melt a little extra butter on the griddle and then ladle the batter by ¼ cupfuls onto the griddle, keeping plenty of space between. Cook about 3-4 minutes until you see bubbles form on the outside. Flip and cook another 1-2 minutes, or until golden brown, and serve.

Top the pancakes with fruit and mascarpone mixture, enjoy! Makes 6-8 pancakes.

Bacon Chocolate Chip Pancakes

Bacon, salt and chocolate make excellent bedfellows. Each ingredient maximizes the flavors of the others. This is truly a match made in heaven.

6 slices center cut bacon
¼ t coarse Kosher salt
2 C all purpose flour
1 T baking powder
½ t salt
1½ T sugar
2 C whole milk
2 eggs
2 T butter, melted, but not hot
1 t vanilla extract
½ C dark chocolate mini morsels

Fry the bacon in a medium pan until quite crispy. Reserve on paper towels and pat off excess fat, then sprinkle with the salt. Break the bacon into bite-sized pieces. Set aside.

Preheat griddle. Sift all the dry ingredients and mix together. Whisk the eggs until they become frothy then mix in all the other wet ingredients. Add the dry ingredients to the wet in small amounts and stir gently. Do not over mix; lumps are perfectly fine. Add the bacon pieces and chocolate morsels to the batter.

Melt a little extra butter on the griddle and then ladle the batter by ¼ cupfuls onto the griddle, keeping plenty of space between. Cook about 3-4 minutes until you see bubbles form on the outside. Flip and cook another 1-2 minutes, or until golden brown, and serve.

Serve with 100% pure maple syrup. Makes 6-8 pancakes.

Buckwheat Pancakes

The lovely dark color is a nice surprise with these pancakes. After giving these a try, many of my friends find they prefer buckwheat pancakes over the traditional type.

COOL TRIVIA: Buckwheat does not contain any wheat. In fact, it is not a grain at all. Related to sorrel and rhubarb, it contains wonderfully healthy grain-like seeds that can be used like wheat flour. (You can make this recipe gluten free by eliminating the regular flour and doubling the amount of buckwheat flour.)

½ C buckwheat flour
½ C all purpose flour
½ t baking soda
1 t baking powder
1 egg plus one yolk, gently beaten
2 t local honey
1⅓ C buttermilk or whole milk
2 T unsalted butter, melted
unsalted butter or grapeseed oil

Mix the dry ingredients together until well blended. In a separate bowl whisk the egg and egg yolk and then add the honey, milk and melted butter. Add the wet ingredients to the dry a little at a time. Do not over mix. Remember, as with all pancake batters, a few lumps are just fine.

Heat a cast iron skillet (or griddle) over medium heat and then melt about ½ T butter or use a little oil to lightly cover the surface. Use about 2 T of batter for each pancake and cook until you begin to see bubbles forming in the batter. Flip the pancake and cook for another 1-2 minutes.

My favorite toppings:
- A handful of blueberries or chopped pecans and maple syrup
- A dollop of creme fraiche and sliced strawberries
- Agave syrup with sliced bananas and a squeeze of fresh lime juice

Timothy's Waffle Mix

2 C all purpose flour

3 t baking powder

½ t sea salt

2 T sugar

2 fresh eggs

1½ C whole milk

4 T unsalted butter, melted

½ t vanilla extract

cooking spray

For me, the best waffles are crisp on the outside and light and fluffy on the inside. To produce this dichotomy of textures takes a bit of practice...and also admittedly, a little luck.

But waffles are so darn good they're worth your time and patience. Remember, practice makes perfect.

Preheat your waffle iron.

Sift the flour and other dry ingredients into a medium-sized bowl. In a separate bowl, whisk the eggs until frothy then add the milk, butter and vanilla, whisk to combine.

Stir the dry ingredients, a little at a time into the wet ingredients and blend them together. Do not over mix, small lumps are fine.

Spray the waffle iron with cooking spray and add the waffle mixture to just cover the surface. Cook until the waffle is done, about 4-5 minutes. NOTE: When you first close the waffle iron a burst of water vapor will be released. When the steam slows, and almost comes to a stop, it is time to check your waffles for color. Are they golden brown? If not cook for 1-2 more minutes and check again...that should be perfect.

Makes 3-4, eight-inch round waffles, or 3, nine-inch square waffles.

My Favorite Waffle Toppings

• Granola & Fresh Berries

• Sliced Strawberries & Creme Fraiche

• Walnuts & Apples (*Use a tart apple like Granny Smith, sliced into ¼" thick wedges. Heat a small saute pan over medium heat. Melt 1 T butter, add the apple slices. Cook until softened, about 5-7 minutes.*)

• Bananas & Nutella (*Top waffles with 1-2 T Nutella; allow to melt a little and then add sliced bananas.*)

Sides

When it comes to a side dish, usually one ingredient is the star. The stars in the following recipes are mainly fruits and vegetables. Their rich tastes and textures complement most any savory dish and round out the presentation with a splash of color.

Any dish tastes best when you use what is fresh (and explaining the many health benefits to eating whole food would require a whole other book!). For now at least, rest assured when it comes to taste, you cannot go wrong selecting what is fresh and in season: Strawberries and asparagus in spring, followed by blackberries and blueberries; then cherries, peaches, zucchini and tomatoes in summer; apples and squash in fall; citrus and root vegetables in winter.

There is nothing better than beginning your weekend with a Saturday morning trip to your local farmers' market where the selection cannot be compared to what you find in most grocery stores. These folks are also a cornucopia of useful information — from growing fruits and vegetables, to storage and even new recipes.

Caramelized Onions

I like to use sweet onions like Vidalia or Walla Walla when caramelizing onions. If you cannot find these varieties, yellow onions will do.

There is only one rule to remember here: Patience is the key. Cook low and slow to develop the inner sweetness of the marvelous onion.

And one more suggestion...not a rule: The easiest way to thinly and uniformly slice onions is to use a mandolin. This nifty device will save you time and yield sliced veggies that any chef would be proud of.

4 large Vidalia onions, peeled, sliced ¼" thick
(use a mandolin!)
2 T unsalted butter
2 T extra virgin olive oil
salt and freshly ground pepper

Heat a large Dutch oven or cast iron skillet over medium heat. Melt the butter and when it stops foaming add the olive oil. Carefully add the onion slices and toss, using tongs to coat all the strands with a little oil. Season the onions with a little salt and pepper and turn the heat to simmer. I'm talking *low* heat here, people. If your range does not have a simmer setting, turn it to its lowest setting and set the Dutch oven partially off the burner. You will have to turn the Dutch oven periodically to brown all the onions. Now cover the Dutch oven and allow it to simmer for about 15 minutes. Check and toss the onions around at this point; cover and cook for an-

other 15 minutes. Total cooking time is usually around a hour, but as I said before, do not be in a hurry; low and slow is the key. The final result will yield slightly browned onions that are soft and sweet. Use some of these caramelized onions for the frittata on page 27; the remainder will keep in the refrigerator for about a week and are great on pizzas or in French onion soup, .

Roasted Red Peppers

Actually you can roast any color bell pepper, I just happen to like the red ones best. This is another easy item to prepare and it has multiple applications. You can use these roasted beauties in a variety of ways, such as the frittata on page 27. They are also great when submerged in olive oil and stored for several weeks.

4 red bell peppers, halved lengthwise, seeded

Preheat broiler to high.

After cleaning the bell peppers, place them on a baking pan, skin side up and about 3 inches from the broiler. Broil the peppers until the skin is black and charred.

The goal is to char the outer skin of the pepper. To help facilitate peeling the charred skin off the underlying roasted pepper, place the peppers in a paper bag and allow the residual steam to help do the work. After about 10-15 minutes in the bag the charred skin will peel off easily, leaving you with beautiful and tasty roasted peppers.

Salsa

INTERESTING SALSA FACT: Salsa dancing originated in New York in the mid-1970s, evolving from the Cha Cha and Mambo. It incorporates swing dancing moves as well as elements from Afro-Cuban and Afro-Caribbean dances.

Some claim salsa dancing is so named because musicians shouted "Salsa!" while they were playing. Others say record labels chose the word because its spicy connotations worked well for marketing purposes.

All I know is, fresh salsa can really spice up a plate of eggs!

1 pint cherry tomatoes, quartered
2 T onions, ¼" dice
1 small clove garlic, diced
juice of one lime
juice of one lemon
salt and pepper, to taste
1 t fresh oregano leaves, chopped
1 T fresh cilantro leaves, chopped

Quarter the tomatoes with a sharp knife so as to slice them, not mash them. A very sharp paring knife or a serrated edge knife works best. Place the tomatoes, diced onions and garlic in a large bowl then add the lemon and lime juice. Toss this a bit to combine. Season the salsa with salt and freshly ground pepper to taste. At this stage allow the flavors to marry for about 15-20 minutes at room temperature. Finally, when you are ready to serve, add the fresh herbs and toss to combine.

For an easy way to make your own tasty chips for dipping see page 150.

Mango Salsa

Add all the ingredients together in a large mixing bowl, except the fresh herbs, and allow the flavors to marry for about 15 minutes. Add the fresh herbs when you are ready to serve.

3 mangos, peeled seeded, ¼" dice

½ red onion, ¼" dice (about ¼ C)

1 jalapeno, ¼" dice (remove the seeds if you like)

¼ bell pepper, ¼" dice (about 2 T), any color pepper will do

1 small clove garlic, minced

2 T freshly squeezed lime juice

1 T fresh parsley or cilantro, chopped

Peach Salsa

Add all ingredients together in a large mixing bowl, except the fresh herbs, and allow the flavors to marry for about 15 minutes. Add the fresh herbs when you are ready to serve.

NOTE: An Anaheim pepper is a mild variety of the New Mexico chile pepper. You can also use poblano peppers.

5-6 firm, but ripe peaches

½ Vidalia onion, ¼" dice (about ¼ C)

1 Anaheim pepper, seeded, ¼" dice

2 T white balsamic vinegar

1 T honey

⅛ t ground cinnamon (optional)

1 T fresh mint, chopped

Zucchini Hash Browns

Here is another wonderful way to use some of the bountiful crop of zucchini that appears near the end of summer. These "hash browns" are light and flavorful, just remember to eat them within about an hour of cooking because they tend to become a little soggy after that point.

2-3 medium zucchini, grated (about 3 C)

½ t Kosher salt

1 farm fresh egg, beaten lightly

¼ C Parmesan cheese, grated

½ t freshly ground pepper

3 T all purpose flour (perhaps a little more)

1 T cornstarch

1 T baking powder

2 T fresh parsley, chopped

2 T unsalted butter

2 T olive oil

Grate the zucchini over a colander and then sprinkle with ½ t salt. Allow the salt to draw the water from the zucchini for about 10-15 minutes. Remove the zucchini to a clean kitchen towel and press to remove any remaining moisture.

Lightly beat the egg in a medium bowl and then add the Parmesan cheese, pepper, flour, cornstarch, baking powder, parsley and season with salt and freshly ground pepper. Whisk to blend. Now add the zucchini and whisk together. You want to create a texture similar to a very thick soup. If the mixture is still too moist, add a bit more flour, one teaspoon at a time. (Don't go crazy here, though.)

Heat half of the butter and oil in a 12-inch, non-stick skillet over medium heat. When the butter stops foaming, place about ¼ C of the zucchini mixture per serving in the prepared skillet, flattening slightly with the back of a large spoon. Cook for about 3 minutes per side or until golden brown. Remove these to a paper towel lined plate and repeat for the rest of the zucchini mixture.

Yields about 6-8 servings. (Can be kept warm in a 200° oven, but are best within an hour of cooking.)

Baked Grapefruit

I wasn't really a fan of grapefruits as a kid, or even as a young adult. Then, while in med school I sampled this dish at a friend's home in Tampa, Florida. After one bite, I absolutely changed my mind!

2 grapefruits
4 t brown sugar
honey

Preheat broiler.

Cut off a small portion of each end of the grapefruit to achieve a flat surface and then cut them in half at their "equator." Using a small, sharp knife section the grapefruits.

Place all 4 grapefruit halves in a baking dish and sprinkle each with 1 t of brown sugar and a small drizzle of honey. Broil these grapefruits in the oven until the sugar is brown and bubbly.

Enjoy!

(4 servings)

Mixed Berry Bowl *with Mascarpone*

1 C mascarpone
1 pint blueberries
1 pint raspberries
1 pint blackberries
1 T freshly squeezed lime juice
zest of one lime
agave syrup or honey

Nothing says summer like a bowl of fresh berries. This combo is not only tasty, but super healthy as well.

Rinse and place the berries in a large mixing bowl.

Add the lime juice and allow the berries to macerate for about 5 minutes.

Meanwhile place a ¼ C of the mascarpone in 4 small bowls. Add the mixed berries and top with a sprinkle of lime zest.

Drizzle just a little honey on top before serving.

Grilled Peaches

GEEKY FRUIT FACT: Peaches and nectarines are so closely related that if you plant 100 peach pits, a few will grow into nectarine trees, and vice versa. What this means is, nectarines are virtually interchangeable with peaches.

To choose great peaches (or nectarines), look for a golden background and a nice fragrance. Ripe fruit has a slight give when squeezed *gently* in your palm. Peaches continue to ripen after they've been picked, so if you have fruit that is slightly firm, just leave it on the counter for a day or two and it will soften and ripen. Do not refrigerate peaches until they are fully ripe or they will end up mealy and tasteless.

4 ripe, but firm peaches, sliced
1 t sugar
2 T honey or agave syrup

Preheat grill to medium and clean the cooking surface well.

In a large mixing bowl, toss the sugar with the sliced peaches.

Grill the peaches for about 2-3 minutes, flip and grill for another 2 minutes.

Drizzle with a little honey and serve.

Mango, Cherry & Mint Salad

Before refrigeration, produce was preserved by pickling it prior to shipping. Those "pickled peppers Peter Piper picked" were also called mangos, as were nearly all fruits and vegetables in those days. In fact, during the 18th century, the word "mango" was used as a verb, meaning "to pickle."

Today, when we say mango, we are talking about a luscious, sweet fruit, best enjoyed fresh!

2 fresh mangos, peeled and cut into 1" cubes
1 lb fresh cherries, pitted and sliced in half
1 T raw sugar
¼ C sweet dessert wine, such as Vin de Glaciere Riesling, Washington State
1 T lemon zest
10 fresh mint leaves

In a large mixing bowl place the fruit and sprinkle with sugar. Toss to combine and allow the fruit to sit for about 10 minutes in the bowl.

Now add the dessert wine and allow this to blend together for another 5 minutes.

Just before serving, sprinkle in the lemon zest and the mint leaves.

Enjoy!

Strawberries *with Balsamic Vinegar*

These berries are great with pancakes, waffles or French toast. (They also make a great addition to vanilla ice cream!)

1 pint fresh strawberries, rinsed, tops removed and cut in half lengthwise.

3 T aged balsamic vinegar

Rinse the berries just before serving (otherwise they will become too soft) and cut in half.

Add the balsamic vinegar and toss to mix together.

Allow the vinegar to marry with the balsamic vinegar for about 10 minutes, then serve.

Baked Apples

I have to thank Chef Andrew Arcovio in Charlotte, North Carolina for this recipe, a favorite of mine for autumn mornings. I like to make these apples just before everyone gets out of bed. The amazing aroma of apples and cinnamon has got to be the best wake up call ever. (If you're not an early riser, make these the night before and then reheat in the morning at 300° for about 15 minutes.)

3-4 apples, such as Fuji or Honeycrisp
zest of one lemon
3 T unsalted butter, melted
¼ C golden raisins
⅓ C brown sugar
1 t cinnamon, freshly grounded is a nice touch
⅛ t allspice, ground
½ C apple cider
juice of ½ lemon
honey to drizzle

Coring apples while leaving the bottom intact (so the filling won't seep out) can be a little tricky. Here's how I do it. Peel the skin from the apple about ½" down from the top. Next, with a sharp paring knife, remove the stem and the top part of the core by placing the blade of the knife about ½" from the center and about ½" deep at about a 45° angle. Then take the apple and turn it around the blade (slowly) until you've gone full circle. Do this one or two more times going a little deeper each time. For the final removal of the core, down near the bottom but not through, I like to use a small melon baller. (This nifty little tool is a bit easier to handle than a knife.)

Melt the butter and remove from heat. Chop the raisins and add them to a small mixing bowl. Add the brown sugar, butter, cinnamon and allspice and mix these all together.

Now fill each cored apple with some of the raisin mixture, about a scant tablespoon each. Place the apples, stuffed side up, in a baking dish. Add the apple cider and lemon juice to the bottom of the dish and drizzle the top of the apples with honey. Bake at 350° for 45 minutes; baste every ten minutes or so.

Remove from the oven and cool for 5-10 minutes. Serve them with another little drizzle of honey on top. Everyone around your breakfast table will thank you!

Prosciutto Wrapped Melon & Figs

This is a simple Italian favorite. It is very refreshing and packs enough protein to keep you content throughout the morning. This dish goes well with a little cheese like fresh mozzarella, Fontina, Brie or manchego.

Prosciutto, unlike pancetta, has been cured and does not need to be cooked before eating. The outside of the ham is usually rubbed with salt and sometimes other spices to draw out moisture while the ham slowly air dries; this process can take a few months to a several years depending on the desired result.

6 slices prosciutto, sliced very thing and quartered
½ cantaloupe, seeds and skin removed, sliced 1-2" or use a melon baller
3 mission figs, sliced in half

Cut each piece of prosciutto into four pieces. Simply wrap some of the cantaloupe pieces with a little piece of prosciutto. You can use a toothpick to hold it together. Repeat this process with the remainder of the melon pieces and all the fig halves. Enjoy on a beautiful sunny morning.

Crispy Hash Browns *with Sauteed Onions, Garlic & Thyme*

Hash browns are the quintessential side dish to pair with "dippy eggs," eggs over easy. I love the crispy texture of the hash browns combined with the runny yellow yolk and soft egg white. Here I've stepped up my plain hash browns with some sauteed onions, a little garlic and fresh thyme. I think these additions take them over the top. However, if you want a potato-only hash brown, just delete the onion, garlic and thyme and follow the rest of the recipe. Also, I use a biscuit cutter here to make a neat disk shape, but this isn't a must do. You can mold about ¼ to ⅓ C of the potato mixture in your hands and then saute them in the pan.

3 russet potatoes, peeled and grated
1 small yellow onion, ¼" dice (about ½ C)
1 clove garlic, minced
3 T unsalted butter, divided
3 T olive oil, divided
2 t fresh thyme, chopped
salt and freshly ground pepper

Peel and grate the potatoes into a bowl of cold water. Place the grated potatoes into a large colander and rinse once more with cold water. Allow them to drain, then place the potatoes into a salad spinner and spin them to release as much water as possible. If you don't have a salad spinner, place on a clean kitchen towel and wring out the excess water.

Heat a large, non-stick skillet over medium heat. Melt 1 T butter and 1 T olive oil in the pan. Add the onion and cook until a light golden brown, stirring frequently. Now add the garlic and cook until fragrant, about 1-2 minutes more. Remove the pan from the heat and place the onions and garlic into a mixing bowl. Combine the grated potatoes with the onions and add the fresh thyme. Stir to combine. Season with salt and pepper.

Return the skillet to medium heat. Add 1 T butter and 1 T olive oil. Place 3-4 biscuit cutters into the pan. Now fill each biscuit cutter with the hash brown mixture and press them down with a silicon spatula or wooden spoon. Cook over medium heat until the bottom turns golden brown. Now flip using a flat spatula and cook this side until golden brown. Serve immediately or remove to a baking sheet and keep them warm in a preheated oven set at 200°. Repeat this process with any remaining potato mixture.

Rosti

I first sampled this potato dish with a few great friends that I had the privilege to meet during my critical care fellowship in Basel, Switzerland.

This classic Swiss dish is strikingly simple and deceptively delish! The key to cooking this crisp dish is to remove as much water from the potatoes as possible before you start to cook them. I have tried many methods but this technique seems to be the easiest and the most consistent.

1 lb Yukon gold potatoes, grated
½ yellow onion, grated
4 T unsalted butter, divided
¼ C canola oil, divided

Place the grated potatoes and onion in a salad spinner and season with a little salt. Spin for one minute. Remove the excess water from the bottom and spin again for another minute. Place the mixture onto a clean kitchen towel and spread in a thin layer. Cover with another clean kitchen towel and press out any remaining liquid.

Heat a 12-inch skillet over medium-high heat. Melt the butter and when the foaming ceases, add the canola oil. Add the potato mixture and spread out thinly, using a fork to separate the potatoes. Cook until the edges turn a little brown and the center remains a little translucent (about 15 minutes) then flip this "pancake," cook for another 5 minutes or until it is crispy and beautiful. The rosti can be made ahead and kept warm on a baking sheet in an oven at 250° for up to 1 hour.

Makes 4 servings

Sweet Potato Hash

The word hash is derived from the French verb *hacher* (to chop) and the dish usually contains meat/potatoes and spices. Rather than the traditional meat and potato hash, this version features sweet potatoes.

I can't say enough good things about sweet potatoes. They are low in sodium and cholesterol and an excellent source of dietary fiber and potassium, vitamin A and C.

6 slices maple cured bacon
2-3 sweet potatoes, peeled and diced ¼"
     (about 4 C)
1 small yellow onion, diced ¼" (about 1 C)
3 T unsalted butter
1 T balsamic vinegar
1 T maple syrup
½ t fresh thyme
salt and pepper to taste

Heat a large skillet over low heat and fry the bacon until crisp. Remove the bacon from the pan, discard the rendered fat and then melt the butter. Saute the potatoes for 10-15 minutes then add the onions and saute for another 5-10 minutes. When the potatoes and onions are browned and cooked through, add the vinegar, syrup and thyme. Season with salt and freshly ground pepper to taste. Add the crumbled bacon pieces into the hash and allow them to warm.

Now enjoy with some farm fresh eggs!

Pommes Timothy

This is a take on a classic French potato dish called Pommes Anna, which consists of thinly sliced potatoes layered in concentric circles and cooked in copious amounts of butter until it is crispy brown and delicious. When complete, it is cut into wedges and served with the main course. I like to serve my version with scrambled eggs with perhaps a little cheese. Russet potatoes are a must here. Their starch content allows them to stick together in perfect formation.

1-2 russet potatoes, scrubbed clean and
  sliced into thin circles (use a mandolin)
3 T unsalted butter
3 T olive oil
1½ t fresh rosemary, chopped
salt and freshly ground pepper

The most important thing to do in this recipe is to slice the potatoes into uniform ⅛" slices. This will allow the potatoes to cook evenly and be finished all at the same time. The rest is quite easy, trust me.

Heat a ten-inch skillet over medium heat. Add 2 T butter in the pan, and when it stops foaming add 2 T olive oil. Now for the fun part. Remove the pan from the heat and start to add the potato pieces one at a time in a circular pattern. Start at the edge of the pan, overlapping each potato slice with the next by one third. Continue until you have made it all the way around the pan. Now start the next layer and move the next layer closer to the center. Continue until the entire bottom of the pan is covered with the potato slices. Season this first layer with salt and freshly ground pepper and about one third of the fresh rosemary. Repeat this process for two more layers, making sure to cover any areas that are bare. Cover the pan, reduce the heat to low and return the pan to the heat. Cook this first side for 10-15 minutes or until it is golden brown. You can check the doneness by simply lifting and edge with a spatula and looking underneath.

To flip the pommes, place a dish almost as wide as the pan on top of the potatoes and then place a clean kitchen towel on top of the plate. With a steady hand, invert the pan onto the plate leaving the potatoes on the dish. Now melt the remaining butter and add the remaining olive oil to the pan and then slide the potatoes from the plate back onto the pan. Cover the pan and cook for another 10-15 minutes or until this second side is golden brown. Slice into four wedges.

Herb's Cheesy Grits

What are grits? To say it simply, crushed corn. Grits are small broken grains of corn that are mashed apart by stone mills. And they are delicious!

Herb and I met in 1986 as interns in Newark, New Jersey. Like me, he loved preparing and enjoying beautiful food. Our philosophies on cooking are the same as our philosophies in medicine: keep your priorities straight and everything else will fall in place. I think you'll like his philosophy on grits, too.

2 C whole milk

1 C chicken broth

1 C filtered water

1 t Kosher salt

1 C coarsely ground yellow grits

4 T unsalted butter

½ C white sharp cheddar cheese, grated

In a medium pan bring the milk, chicken broth, water and salt to a boil. Slowly add the cornmeal and whisk together. When all the cornmeal is incorporated, turn the heat to simmer and partially cover the pot. Stir this mixture every 4-5 minutes until the cornmeal has absorbed the liquids and has become smooth. Remove this from the heat, add the butter and mix to combine. Season to taste with salt and freshly ground pepper.

Just before serving, stir in the cheese. Then enjoy immediately. (If the grits become a little too thick, return the pan to low heat, stir and add 1-2 T whole milk.)

Grits *with Onion, Bacon & Jalapeno*

4 slices of center cut bacon

1 small yellow onion, ¼" dice

2 C whole milk

½ C fresh corn, removed from the cob

1 C chicken broth

1 C filtered water

1 t kosher salt

1 C coarsely ground yellow grits

4 T unsalted butter

½ C white sharp cheddar cheese, grated

1 jalapeno, seeded and diced ¼"

2 dashes Tabasco sauce

1 T fresh parsley (or cilantro), chopped

Being from Pittsburgh, I did not grow up eating grits. But when I started school in Florida, this creamy, sometimes cheesy, cornmeal quickly became one of my favorite breakfast dishes.

Grits are at their creamiest just after they are cooked. However, they can be covered after cooling, and placed in the refrigerator for up to two days. Just reconstitute them with about 1/4 C water when reheating.

Cook the bacon slices in a medium skillet over low to medium-low heat until crispy. Remove the bacon slices and chop into pieces and reserve. Then add the onion and corn to the rendered bacon fat and saute until glistening (about 5 minutes).

For the grits, bring the milk, chicken broth, water and salt to a boil In a medium sauce pan. Slowly add the cornmeal and whisk together. When all the cornmeal is incorporated turn the heat to simmer and partially cover the pot. Stir this mixture every 4-5 minutes until the cornmeal has absorbed the liquid and has become smooth. Remove from heat, add the butter and mix to combine. Stir in the cheese and add the onions, bacon bits and corn. Add the jalapeno and Tabasco and stir to combine. Serve with a sprinkle of chopped parsley or fresh cilantro.

Spicy Turkey Sausage Patties

1 lb ground turkey

¼ C bread crumbs, unseasoned

1 small yellow onion, chopped ¼"

¼ C fresh parsley, chopped

2 T fresh thyme, chopped

1 T fresh basil, chopped

2 cloves garlic, minced

1 t kosher salt

freshly ground black pepper

1 T chili powder

¼ t cayenne pepper

1 egg, lightly beaten

2-3 T canola oil

As you have probably noticed, I'm not a vegetarian. (Not that there is anything wrong with that!) This is one of my favorite healthy choice meat recipes. I usually make these patties in bulk, vacuum pack 2-4 at a time, and store them in the freezer. They will keep for up to 3 months.

Mix all the ingredients (except the oil) in a large mixing bowl. Note that you may not need all the egg. Add half of the beaten egg and then mix together. You want a texture that is moist enough to work with but not as wet as a meatball. The secret here is to make sure you do not over mix as this will make the patties chewy. Just mix the ingredients enough to bring everything together. Form the meat into 10 patties about ¼" thick. Work in two batches.

Heat half the oil in a ten-inch saute pan on medium-high heat. Brown both sides of the sausage, about 3-4 minutes per side. Remove to a plate lined with a paper towel.

Serve on a biscuit with a little jalapeno jam!

Chicken Sausage

We are fortunate to be able to purchase high quality chicken sausage in most major grocery stores today. But wouldn't it be more fun to go to your local farmers' market and purchase their ground chicken then go home and make some yourself? My only words of advice are to use ground chicken from both the dark and white meat, not the chicken breast alone. For one, the dark meat adds a delicious flavor that can't be found in white meat alone. And second, by using the whole chicken we might just stop the crazy farming practice of producing chickens with breasts that look like they visited a plastic surgeon.

1 small yellow onion, ¼" dice (about ½ C)

1-2 T olive oil

1 lb ground chicken

¼ C fresh bread crumbs

1 farm fresh egg, lightly beaten

2 t rubbed sage

1 T fresh rosemary, chopped

1 t fennel seed

1 t salt and freshly ground pepper

Heat a medium saute pan and saute the onion in the olive oil. Remove from the heat and allow to cool. Combine the chicken, onion and bread crumbs and then the egg. Note that you may not need all the egg. Add half of the beaten egg and then mix together. Using your fingers, blend these ingredients together thoroughly. Now add the spices, season with salt and pepper and mix together.

Form the "sausage" into small balls and then flatten into patties about 3" round and ½" thick. The patties are ready to cook now but they will hold together better if you allow them to rest in the refrigerator for several hours or overnight.

You may saute these patties in your choice of oil over medium heat until golden brown on both sides. They may also be individually wrapped, vacuum packed and frozen for up to three months.

Maple Pepper Bacon

There is something special about the combination of bacon, maple syrup and freshly ground pepper. If you do not have a high quality pepper grinder, go buy one right now! The flavors release by using freshly ground pepper are so much richer. You will never use ground black pepper again and you will enjoy the freshly ground pepper in many of your kitchen creations.

1 lb center cut bacon
2 T pure maple syrup
freshly ground pepper

Preheat oven to 375°.

Line a baking sheet with parchment paper. Bake the bacon for 15 minutes in the preheated oven. Remove the pan from the oven, flip the bacon and pat dry with paper towels. Brush the bacon with the maple syrup and then sprinkle well with the freshly ground pepper. Bake an additional 10-15 minutes until just crisp.

Corned Beef Hash

This is absolutely one of my favorite breakfast foods. I make my hash more memorable by adding a little extra spice and some fresh herbs. Serve it with an egg or two, over medium and when the yolks are released — awesome!

¾ lb corned beef, ¼" dice
1½ lb Idaho potatoes, peeled, ½" dice
1 yellow onion, ¼" dice
½ red bell pepper, ¼" dice
1 clove garlic, minced
3 T unsalted butter
1-2 T canola oil
1 t Dijon mustard
½ t fresh rosemary

Melt 1 T butter in a 12-inch saute pan over medium heat. Add the diced corned beef and saute until lightly browned then remove to a bowl. Melt the remaining 3 T of butter and the canola oil and then add the potatoes. Cook the potatoes, stirring for 10-15 minutes so that they are evenly dispersed on the pan and starting to brown slightly. Add the onion and red bell pepper and cook for another 5 minutes.

Finally add the garlic, mustard and rosemary, stir to evenly distribute and then add the reserved corned beef. Cook for another 5-10 minutes or until the potatoes are slightly crunchy on the edges and the corned beef is warmed through.

Drinks

The following recipes are perfect when you're looking for a little umph before a workout or something special to sip over brunch.

Smoothies have always been one of my favorite ways to start the day. Their refreshing taste (as well as the vitamins and minerals they pack) can really get you off on the right foot. If a smoothie has to sustain you for several hours, be sure to add a little protein like yogurt, milk (almond or soy if you like) or protein powder.

A couple of great combos: Very Berry Smoothies with a Carolina Blonde & Green Omelet; Tropical Mango Smoothie and Yvette's Scrambled Eggs with Fresh Herbs; or Bryan's Beach Boy Avocado Omelet with a Sparkling Pomegranate & Ginger Cocktail.

Not that I advocate for cocktails first thing in the morning, but when having a few friends for brunch, I like to pair Breakfast Margaritas with Jimi's Huevos Rancheros; or for an Italian flair, a batch of Pear & Thyme Bellinis with a Caprese Style Omelet.

Go Green Smoothie

Going green has never been so easy! All you need is a quality juicing machine.

Before making your purchase, consider the machine's ease of use and especially its ease of cleaning. (This is a machine you will grow to love and use often, so quality does matter.)

2 C fresh cucumber, chopped
1 C fresh spinach leaves, rinsed
1 C Granny Smith apple, cored and seeded
1 C celery
½ C organic white grape juice

Juice each ingredient and then combine with the grape juice in a blender. If you do not have a juicer, you can make this in a blender. A high quality blender such as the Vitamix works best.

Makes two, 8 oz. servings.

Tropical Mango Smoothie

I try to buy only a few bananas at a time. Sometimes, however, they get overripe before I can use them. When this happens, I peel them, cut them in half, cover them with plastic wrap and freeze them for future use, like this smoothie.

8 oz. ice
¼ C lite coconut milk
¼ C orange juice
⅓ C fresh mango, chopped
½ frozen (or fresh) banana
mint sprig

Blend all ingredients together until smooth and creamy. Makes a single serving.

Chuck's Preworkout Smoothie

Smoothies can make for a healthy start to your day, or a preworkout power up, a great healthy treat to enjoy any-time of the day. I have only one piece of advice: First, buy a quality blender. You'll use this for more than just smoothies and it will last for many years. I like the Vitamix brand (as do all the smoothie places in town). I have had mine for close to twenty years and it is still going strong.

8 oz. 1% chocolate milk, cold
1 oz. vanilla whey protein
¼ C blueberries
1 T chia seeds
1 T raw chocolate
½ C rolled oats
3-4 ice cubes

Place all ingredients in a high quality blender and mix until creamy and smooth. If the mixture gets too thick add a little extra liquid (orange juice, coconut milk or even filtered water), 1 tablespoon at a time until you achieve the texture you crave. Garnish with a mint sprig. Makes a single serving.

Hecktor's Banana Protein Smoothie

During our residency, Tony Diaz and I used to workout at Hecktors in Tampa, Florida. Hecktor, the owner of the gym, made some fantastic smoothies. In fact, I think I looked forward to his smoothies more than the workouts.

½ banana, frozen
1 scoop vanilla protein powder
1/2 C skim milk
¼ C vanilla low fat yogurt
¼ t vanilla extract
½ C ice

Blend all ingredients together until smooth and creamy. Makes a single serving.

Very Berry Smoothie

When fruit is at its freshest and most plentiful remember to freeze some for future smoothie use. I like to vacuum seal mine in individual servings, but freezer bags work well too. Just keep in mind, for optimal taste, about 3 months is the max freezer time.

1½ C frozen (or fresh) mixed berries (straw-
berries, blueberries, raspberries)
½ C low fat plain yogurt
1 C organic apple juice
¼ C ice
1 T honey
1 scoop soy protein powder

Blend all ingredients together until smooth and creamy. Makes a single serving.

Watermelon, Cucumber & Basil Cooler

There is no better way to stave off summer's incredible heat than by sipping a cool and refreshing beverage. Here I've combined a couple of summer's favorites, watermelon, cucumber and fresh basil, and made them into a very cool drink. The addition of lime for a little punch and agave syrup for some sweetness rounds this cooler off nicely. Watermelon and cucumbers taste like summer!

4 C fresh watermelon, peeled and seeded, chopped in chunks
2 C fresh English cucumber (hothouse/seedless), peeled, chopped in chunks
¼ C filtered water
1 T agave syrup (optional)
8 fresh basil leaves
2 T freshly squeezed lime juice
1 liter sparkling water (like Pellegrino)
mint sprigs, for garnish

Combine the watermelon and cucumber chunks in a blender and blend on low for one minute. Then add the water, agave syrup and lime juice and blend for another minute or two.

Strain this mixture into a serving pitcher and add the sparkling water.

Serve in glasses (with or without ice) and garnish with a mint sprig.

Sparkling Ginger Pomegranate Cooler

This combination is nice and refreshing and with the little added spice of the fresh ginger — who needs alcohol!

½ C filtered water
2" piece fresh ginger, peeled and cut into long
   thin slices
4 oz. pomegranate juice
1 qt. sparkling water
1-2 T agave syrup
4 mint sprigs, optional

Heat the water in a small pot over medium heat. Add the fresh ginger slices and bring to a low simmer. Remove the pot from the heat and allow the ginger to seep for 10-15 minutes. Strain the ginger water and pour to a large serving pitcher. Then add the pomegranate juice and sparkling water.

Serve in a tall glass packed with ice, garnish with a mint sprig.

Serves 4-6.

Good Morning Margarita

Let's just get this clear, I'm not advocating that you start your day with a nice stiff drink. However, on special occasions this may just hit the spot.

1½ oz. Silver Tequila
½ oz. Grand Marnier
4 oz. (½ C) freshly squeezed grapefruit juice
2 dashes grenadine
ice
lime and orange wedges for garnish

In a cocktail shaker combine the tequila, Grand Marnier and grapefruit juice. Fill a glass with crushed ice and add the dashes of grenadine and then pour in the tequila mixture.

Garnish with a lime and orange wedge.

Serves 1.

Pear Thyme Bellini

Bellinis are traditionally made with fresh peach juice at Harry's Bar in Venice.

Here I've changed the classic drink up a bit by using pear nectar and kissing it with a little fresh thyme. Aah, *delizioso*!

4 oz. pear nectar, chilled

16 oz. (2 C) Prosecco, chilled

4 pear slices, paper thin

8 sprigs thyme, reserve four for garnish

In a large pitcher mix the pear juice and the thyme. Using a muddler, lightly crush the thyme to release its oil and fragrance into the pear juice. Let this steep for about an hour. Strain the liquid to remove the thyme and then refrigerate for at least an hour. Cold is good. When you are ready to serve, add the Prosecco and pour into individual glasses. Garnish each glass with a small twig of thyme and slice of pear.

Serves 4

Jeff Boardman's Totally Bloody Mary

In my little town of Davidson, North Carolina Jeff Boardman makes the best Bloody Mary ever...I'm talking epic here. Please give this a whirl for your next tailgate party, brunch get together...or hell, just for any given Sunday.

1 lime wedge

1 t celery seed

1 T Himalayan rock salt (or kosher salt)

2 oz. premium vodka

4 oz. tomato juice

½ oz. freshly squeezed lemon juice

1 pinch cayenne pepper

3-4 grinds fresh black pepper

1 splash Worcestershire

1 splash Tabasco

1 splash A-1

GARNISH:

lemon peel

Tuscan table olives

cornichons

peperoncini

Run the lime wedge around the rim of an 8-oz. glass. Press the rim of the glass in a mixture of celery seed and rock salt. Fill glass with crushed ice.

In a shaker, mix the vodka, tomato juice, lemon juice, cayenne pepper, black pepper, Worcestershire, Tabasco and A-1. Shake vigorously, several times, then pour into the prepared glass.

Skewer the garnish and rest on the rim of the glass. Enjoy!!

Serves 1

Specialties

The recipes that follow are a little more ambitious. My promise to you: If you spend the time, making sure to practice *Mise en Place*, these recipes will be more than worth the effort.

Breakfast and brunch are a little more intimate than afternoon cocktails or dinner parties. So my suggestion is to keep the atmosphere informal and friendly. Have plenty of fresh coffee and tea available for your guests. (In my kitchen, it's not uncommon for folks to sip espresso while I cook.) Or, even better, have a good sparkling wine ready, like a well-chilled Prosecco.

Also, use small plates because remember: Variety, not volume, is your friend here.

Eggs Timothy

Here is one of my favorite egg dishes, a healthier take on eggs Benedict, but just as delicious.

(If you've ever wondered how the dish eggs Benedict came to be, here's one theory. In a 1942 interview in *The New Yorker*, Lemuel Benedict, a retired Wall Street stock broker, said he'd wandered into the Waldorf Hotel one morning in 1894 requesting a hangover cure. The chef produced a dish of poached eggs on toast with a "hooker" of Hollandaise, and named it for Benedict.)

4 pieces of pancetta, sliced very thin
2 cups fresh spinach, washed and large stems removed
1 small shallot, finely diced
1 T unsalted butter
4 pieces crusty French bread, lightly toasted, ½" thick
4 poached eggs
4 T Fontina cheese, grated
lemon aioli (recipe follows)
fresh thyme for garnish

Preheat broiler to high.

Line a baking sheet with foil.

Heat a 12-inch skillet over medium heat. Add the pancetta and cook until crisp, remove and reserve.

In the same pan, melt the butter and then saute the shallot until fragrant and glistening. Add the spinach and saute, turning frequently with kitchen tongs, until the spinach is wilted and the water is mostly cooked out. Very important here: Spinach has a lot of water, so cook it well but do not crisp it. Set the cooked spinach aside.

Toast the French bread and then smear a little lemon aioli (page 125) on each piece. Place a piece of pancetta on top and then add a small layer of spinach. Now place a poached egg on top and finish with a sprinkle of cheese. Season the eggs with salt and freshly ground pepper. Broil on a lined baking sheet until the cheese is melted and slightly browned. Garnish with fresh thyme.

Serves two, but can be multiplied with ease.

Lemon Aioli

Isn't aioli just a fancy name for mayo, you ask.

Not at all! Aioli hails from the southern French region of Provence, and begins with a mortar and pestle and several cloves of garlic. When the garlic is pounded to a paste, it's whisked into the traditional preparation of egg yolk, lemon juice, mustard and olive oil.

1 egg yolk, use pasteurized eggs if available
1 small garlic clove, mashed
zest of 1 lemon
2 T freshly squeezed lemon juice
½ t Dijon mustard
pinch of cayenne pepper
kosher salt to taste
1 C very light olive oil (or other mild oil)

Whisk the first 6 ingredients in a medium bowl. Add a little salt and continue to whisk to combine. Now rest for a minute.

Begin to whisk again and then slowly, very, very slowly begin to add the oil a little drizzle at a time. Whisk to combine and again, go slow. Once the emulsion starts to come together you can add the oil a little faster...but don't get in a hurry here.

Taste and adjust seasoning as needed. You can store the aioli covered and refrigerated for about a week.

Lobster Benedict

And here's another eggs Benedict theory: A recipe for eggs Benedict appeared in Chef Ranhofer's 1894 cookbook, *The Epicurean,* which includes "a selection of interesting bills of fare of Delmonico's from 1862-1894," in particular a recipe for eggs Benedict, prepared by Ranhofer at Delmonico for Captain and Mrs. Le Grand Benedict who were frequent diners there.

IMPORTANT NOTE: DO NOT OVERCOOK THE LOBSTER! When overcooked, shellfish, lobster included, becomes rubbery. Poach the lobster slowly, over low heat and remove it from the heat before it is completely cooked. Residual heat will finish the cooking process.

2 small lobster tails, cleaned and cut into 4 long
  pieces
4 wooden skewers
2 T unsalted butter
4 poached eggs (see page 2)
2 croissant, halved lengthwise
¼ C hollandaise sauce (page 129)
10 arugula leaves, rinsed, large stems re-
  moved
thyme leaves, separated from their stems
6 finely sliced pieces of truffle

To remove the lobster meat, split the shell in half lengthwise with a sharp, heavy knife. Tear the shell at the bottom perpendicular to the first cut. Now grab the lobster meat and pull it straight up and out of the shell. If it does not release on its own, simply cut the meat from the shell with a knife.

Trim both sides of the lobster meat lengthwise and then split the meat into two long cylinders. When you finish both lobster tails, you should have four long pieces. To keep the meat from curling while cooking, run a wooden skewer lengthwise through the center of each piece of lobster.

Poach 4 eggs (page 2) and place them on a clean plate. Cover with foil to keep warm.

Make hollandaise sauce (page 129) and keep warm in an insulated coffee mug or thermos.

Melt the butter in a large saute pan over low heat. Once the butter stops foaming, add the skewered meat to the pan and saute until the first side is opaque. Flip the meat to the other side, cover the pan and turn off the heat. Stop for a moment

here because this is important. All shellfish, lobster included, can be easily overcooked. When overcooked, it becomes rubbery and inedible. So, DO NOT OVERCOOK THE LOBSTER. It is always best to poach the lobster slowly over low heat and to remove it from the heat just before it is completely cooked through. The residual heat in the meat will finish the cooking process for you. Keep the lobster meat in this pan until you are ready to assemble. Place on a clean plate.

Drain remaining liquid and reheat the pan over medium heat. Add the croissant halves, sliced side down and allow them to toast slightly.

Now to assemble, place 2 halves of the croissant on a warmed plate. Remove the skewers from the meat and place a piece of meat on each croissant half. Add a poached egg to each piece and then drizzle with hollandaise sauce. Garnish with the fresh arugula, thyme and then top with a few truffle slices. Serve immediately.

Serves 2.

Hollandaise Sauce

This sauce used to be difficult for me to make as it was prone to separate. Now I use a Vitamix blender to combine the ingredients and just keep the sauce warm either in a double boiler or a thermos, until serving.

1 stick unsalted butter (8 T)
3 large egg yolks, pasteurized if available
1-2 T freshly squeezed lemon juice
½ t salt
¼ t dry mustard

Melt the butter over low heat in a non-stick pan. Remove the pan from the heat and remove as much of the milk protein (the flaky white stuff) that you can. (This is called clarifying the butter.) Set this aside, but keep warm enough to remain as a liquid.

Combine the egg yolks, lemon juice, salt and dry mustard in the blender and begin to mix on low. Drizzle in the butter very slowly and allow the mixture to thicken. Add salt or lemon juice to taste. Place the sauce in either a double boiler, set on very low, or put into a thermos that will keep it warm. Use as soon as possible.

Low Country Shrimp & Grits

I fell in love with shrimp and grits on one of many trips to Charleston, South Carolina. I've sampled countless versions throughout the country from the best restaurants to the dives. In this version, I use a pseudo seafood stock, combining chicken broth with shrimp shells and heads… don't skip this step, it really adds to the flavor. Shrimp and grits is great for breakfast, as an appetizer, or for dinner.

Buy shrimp by the count, not by the size. The numbers 21-25 mean there are 21-25 shrimp per pound. The larger the number, the smaller the shrimp.

1 lb large (21-25 count) head-on shrimp, head-on shrimp, peeled to the tail and de-veined, shells and heads reserved (you can use 26-30 count too)
1 T Cajun seasoning (like Emeril's Essence)
1 t lemon zest

SHRIMP BROTH
2 C chicken broth
reserved shrimp shells and heads

GRITS
1 C stone ground yellow grits
3 C half and half
1 C water
¼ t salt
1 T unsalted butter

(con't on page 132)

Clean and de-vein the shrimp, reserving shells. Sprinkle shrimp with Cajun seasoning and the lemon zest and set aside.

To make the "shrimp broth," bring the chicken broth to a boil in a medium-sized pot. Now add the reserved shrimp shells to the broth. Cover the pot and reduce heat to low to create a gentle boil. Simmer until reduced by half, about 20-30 minutes. Strain the broth into a bowl making sure to press the shells to extract all their goodness, keep it warm and set aside.

To make the grits: In a saucepan, bring the half and half, water and salt to a gentle boil, add the grits and immediately reduce the heat to low. Simmer uncovered, stirring occasionally, until most of the liquid has been absorbed (about 10-12 minutes). When the grits come to the right consistency (moist but with most of the liquid absorbed) add the butter and stir to blend well, keep warm.

(con't page 132)

Ingredients, con't from page 131:

3 strips bacon
¼ C andouille sausage, ¼" dice
1 T olive oil
1 shallot, ¼" dice
½ green bell pepper, ¼" dice
1 clove garlic, minced

ROUX
2 T unsalted butter
2 T all purpose flour, unbleached

1 T lemon juice
2 T scallions, about 1" of the green and all the white, chopped

In a 12-inch skillet cook bacon over medium-low heat until crispy. Remove the bacon strips and set aside. Remove all but 1 T of the rendered bacon fat and saute the andouille sausage until it is slightly browned, reserve in a bowl. Remove most of the rendered fat and add 1 T olive oil to the pan. Now saute the shallot, bell pepper and garlic until translucent, about 6 minutes. Remove this to a bowl.

Melt 1 T of the butter over medium-low heat and when it stops foaming, saute the shrimp until almost cooked through. You want to slightly undercook them. (You will finish cooking them later.) Remove to a separate plate.

Melt the remaining 2 T butter and when it stops foaming, add the flour, a little at a time, and continuously stir. Yes, we are making a roux, so put the cell phone down and don't let your attention drift away from this flavor making process. Stir the roux frequently, very frequently, until it turns a caramel color. Watch the roux go from white, to blonde, to light brown, and then to caramel…it's a beautiful thing.

Now slowly add the warm "shrimp broth", a little at a time, to the roux. Stir to prevent lumps from forming. Keep stirring until it achieves a thick, fluid consistency. (The mixture should be able to coat the back of a spoon.)

Crumble the bacon into the roux and add all of the other sauteed ingredients. Stir in the lemon juice and add the shrimp to complete its cooking. This should only take a minute or two.

To serve, place a ¼ C of grits onto a plate and top with 3-5 shrimp (depending on size). Drizzle a little of the brown sauce on top of the shrimp and a little beside the grits, garnish with scallions or parsley and serve immediately.

Serves 4.

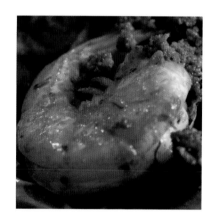

Crab Cakes, *for breakfast?*

Okay, I admit crab is one of my absolute favorite foods so I find reasons to eat it anytime of day.

I've heard time and time again that this recipe makes the best crab cakes ever — you be the judge. These are great with a little remoulade, page 137.

1 lb lump crab meat, rinsed and picked
   through for shells
½ medium yellow onion, ¼" dice
½ red bell pepper, ¼" dice
1 stalk celery, ¼" dice
½ C fresh bread crumbs
½ C mayonnaise
1 T Dijon mustard
1 t Worcestershire
1 egg
1 t fresh thyme, chopped fine
1 T fresh parsley, finely chopped
zest of one lemon
salt and pepper to taste
1 C panko bread crumbs
3 T unsalted butter

Combine all the ingredients (except the panko and butter) in a large mixing bowl and combine gently. If you have true lump crab meat, leave most of the large chunks intact but do break up a couple of the pieces. This will make forming and holding the crab cake together much easier. The large pieces will add to the drama and will be much appreciated when served. Form the crab mixture into 6-8 patties. I like to wet my hands when I form the patties; it helps to keep the cakes together. For best results, refrigerate the patties for 2 hours or overnight; this process also helps them stay together better.

When you are ready to cook the crab cakes, place the panko bread crumbs on a large plate and lightly coat each side of the patty. Season with salt and pepper if you like.

In a large, non-stick saute pan, melt the butter over medium-low heat and when it stops foaming saute the crab patties until golden brown. Flip patties with a spatula, trying not to let them break apart (which I admit is sometimes difficult). To make the flipping process a little easier, try not to overcrowd the crab cakes in the pan. Work in batches if necessary. You can keep the crab cakes warm by placing them on a baking sheet in a preheated oven set at 250°.

Makes 4-6 servings.

Breakfast Salmon Patties

Perhaps your memories of salmon cakes are like mine. Mom made them with canned salmon and a little mayonnaise, and served them on Wonder Bread.

Let me tell you, these are not Mama's salmon cakes! This combination of fresh herbs and veggies, along with a little Dijon, horseradish and Worcestershire sauce, really steps up the flavor. Don't let fresh salmon intimidate you. It's easy to work with and oh so tasty.

1 shallot, ¼" dice, sauted

2 leeks, chopped, rinsed (all the white part and some of the green)

3 T canola oil, divided

1½ lb fresh salmon, skin removed

1 egg, slightly beaten

⅓ C fresh bread crumbs

1 T Dijon mustard

½ t Worcestershire sauce

2 T fresh parsley, chopped

1 t horseradish sauce

Saute the shallots and leeks in 1 T oil until fragrant. Season with salt and freshly ground pepper and allow this to cool. Put the salmon in a food processor and chop briefly to a 1/4" dice. Combine the salmon with all the other ingredients and mix gently. Cover with plastic wrap and place in the refrigerator for at least 1 hour, or overnight.

Remove the salmon mixture from the refrigerator and form small patties about ¼ C in volume and place on a piece of parchment paper.

Heat a 12-inch, non-stick saute pan on medium and add 2 T oil. Saute the salmon patties, forming a golden crust, about 3-4 minutes per side.

I like to serve salmon patties with remoulade, fresh greens and some fresh fruit.

Serves 4

Remoulade

Remoulade, though invented in France, is a popular condiment in many countries. Very much like the tartar sauce of some English-speaking cultures, it is typically served with seafood. However, in Belgium it is the go to sauce for *pomme frites* and in Denmark, they pair it with roast beef.

To make this sauce, just mix everything together and chill in the fridge.

¼ C mayonnaise

1 t horseradish

1½ t Dijon mustard

2 dashes Worcestershire

2 dashes Tabasco

1 t Emeril's Essence or other Cajun seasoning

1 t fresh parsley, chopped

½ t white wine vinegar

1 t ketchup

Breakfast Quesadilla *with Gulf Shrimp & Salsa*

Fresh shrimp is ideal here. However, if you don't live near the coast, you can use frozen shrimp. And though I usually cook 21-25 count shrimp (meaning 20-25 shrimp per pound), in this recipe I like to use 36-40 count shrimp. These shrimp are much smaller and just look so cute nestled in a tortilla.

3 T unsalted butter, divided
½ yellow onion, ¼" dice
1 small clove garlic, diced
1 C diced fresh tomatoes
1 T fresh oregano leaves, chopped
1 T fresh cilantro leaves, chopped
1 t lemon zest

½ lb, 36-40 count gulf shrimp, peeled and deveined
salt and freshly ground pepper
6 large eggs
2 T milk
4, 8-inch flour tortillas
4 t cream cheese, room temperature

To make the "salsa," heat a large, non-stick skillet over medium heat. Melt 1 T butter and then saute the onion until translucent. Add the garlic and cook until fragrant, about another minute. Add the tomatoes and cook for 1-2 more minutes, just to soften. Remove the pan from the heat and add the herbs and lemon zest. Place in a bowl and reserve.

Melt 1 T butter into the pan and saute the shrimp until just cooked through, about 3 minutes. Season with a little salt and pepper and place them in a separate bowl.

Gently whisk the eggs and half and half together, and season with salt and freshly ground pepper. Now, using the same pan, melt the other 1 T of butter, this time on low heat, and gently scramble the eggs until soft and luxurious.

To assemble the quesadillas, spread 1 t cream cheese on each tortilla. Add a layer of scrambled eggs then a layer of shrimp and top with half of the salsa. Top with another tortilla, cream cheese side down. (Makes 2 quesadillas.)

Place the quesadillas in the pan. On medium-low heat, slightly brown one side. Then flip the quesadilla, by placing a slightly smaller plate over the pan. Place a kitchen towel over the plate and gently turn the pan, moving the quesadilla onto the plate. Slide the quesadilla back into the pan and cook until golden brown. Transfer to a cutting board and slice into 4 wedges. Repeat for the remaining quesadilla. (Makes 2 quesadillas, or 8 wedges.)

Breakfast Quesadilla *with Chorizo Sausage*

Chorizo sausage hails from Spain's Iberian Peninsula. It gets its distinctive smokiness and deep red color from dried smoked red peppers. Traditionally, chorizo is encased in natural casings, a method used since Roman times.

2 T unsalted butter

½ yellow onion, diced

3 large eggs, whipped

1 T half and half

¼ C cheddar cheese, grated

6 oz. chorizo sausage, crumbled

4, 9-inch corn tortillas

cooking spray

12 cherry tomatoes, quartered

1 small jalapeno, seeds removed and diced fine

1 T cilantro, rinsed and chopped

¼ C cheddar cheese, grated

Melt the butter in a large skillet. When the butter stops foaming, add the onions and saute until they are translucent (about 3 minutes). Scramble the eggs and half and half and begin to cook them slowly. Season the eggs with salt and pepper and add the cheese. When the eggs are set, but not dry, remove to a separate plate and reserve.

Wipe the pan clean with a paper towel and return to the burner. Add the crumbled chorizo and cook thoroughly. Remove to paper towels to soak up the rendered fat and reserve.

Spray the pan with cooking spray and then return it to the burner on low heat. Add one tortilla and then cover with half of the cheesy eggs, half the chorizo and half the tomatoes, jalapenos, cilantro and half the extra cheddar cheese. Top this with another tortilla and cook on low for about 2 minutes, lightly browning one side. To flip the quesadilla, place a slightly smaller plate over the pan, covering the tortilla. Place a kitchen towel over the plate, and gently turn the pan, moving the quesadilla onto the plate. Slide the quesadilla back into the pan and cook for another 2 minutes or until the tortilla is golden brown. Transfer to a cutting board and slice into wedges. Repeat for the remaining quesadilla.

Makes 2 quesadillas, or 8 wedges.

From Austin, with Migas

This dish of eggs, crispy tortillas and sofrito is a Tex-Mex staple for the great folks in Austin, Texas. The secret, I've found, is to make your own crispy chips by pan-frying corn tortillas. (For those who are a little less ambitious, store bought corn tortilla chips will do just fine.)

Migas means crumbs in Spanish, and I guarantee there won't be any crumbs left at your breakfast table when you serve this dish!

FOR THE CRISP TORTILLA CHIPS:
3, 6" corn tortillas, cut into ½" strips
1 C canola oil
good quality chili powder
FOR THE EGGS:
4 T unsalted butter, divided
½ yellow onion, ¼" dice
½ green bell pepper ¼"dice
1 clove garlic, minced
3-4 plum tomatoes, chopped
1 jalapeno, seeded, diced (optional)
8 large eggs, gently beaten until foamy
3 T half and half
salt and freshly ground pepper
1 C Monterey Jack cheese, shredded
3 T fresh cilantro, chopped

Place the oil in a large Dutch oven. The oil should be about ½" in depth. Heat the oil over medium high to a temperature of 350° (check with a candy thermometer). Add a few strips of tortilla, working in batches so as not to overcrowd, and fry lightly on both sides turning with tongs a few times (about 3 minutes total). Remove the tortilla strips to a paper towel lined plate and lightly sprinkle with chili powder. Reserve.

Heat a 12-inch, non-stick saute pan over medium heat. Melt 2 T of butter and when the foaming ceases, saute the onion and bell pepper until softened and glistening (about 5 minutes). Then add the garlic and saute until fragrant (about 2 minutes more). Finally add the tomatoes and jalapeno and saute for another 2 minutes. Remove the pan from the heat and place the veggie mixture in a bowl to reserve.

Return the pan to the cooktop and turn the temperature to medium low. Melt 1 T butter until foaming. Meanwhile, whisk the eggs and half and half together. It is best to cook the eggs in two batches. Place half of the eggs in the pan and add half the veggies. Slowly turn and fold the eggs until cooked about halfway through. Then add half of the cheese, season with salt and pepper and add about half of the tortilla chips. When the eggs are cooked through, divide onto two plates, garnish with cilantro and serve. Repeat with remaining eggs, veggies and cheese for two additional servings.

Serves 4

143

ACKNOWLEDGMENTS

To my food stylist and editor Leslie Rindoks and my photographer Kurt Rindoks for first and foremost believing in my craft, and making even my average dishes look spectacular.

To Steve Malingowski, my chef mentor who taught me how to crack my first egg, not to mention just about everything else I know about cooking.

To Judy and Chuck Latham for their enduring friendship. Only true friends would allow me to destroy their kitchen for a final photo shoot. Judy's eclectic collection of plates and bowls and glasses made a world of difference to the appearance of my book. They are my favorite people to share a meal with, something I hope will continue for many years to come.

THE CREW: Leslie Rindoks, Judy Latham, Chuck Latham, Kurt Rindoks, Yvette Harrold, Timothy O'Lenic and Hank

To the Davidson gang: Edie and Doug Surratt, Katie and Tim Barker, Catherine and Henry Boardman, Bonnie and Jeff Boardman, Jodie and Mike Silver, Pam and Andy Hansen and Pat Peroni, the best neighbors and test kitchen staff anyone could ask for. Thanks for enjoying my cooking triumphs and enduring the failures. And thanks to Mary Jane Walters who raided her kitchen cupboards to find the perfect plate.

To Amy Schneider and Paul Kritzer for introducing me to my better half — here's to experimenting with more new recipes!

To my California family, Chris Anne, Lindsay, Danny, Tom O'Lenic and Bryan Wilson — surf's up people, but let's have breakfast, first!

To my Florida family, Amanda, Austin and Bill O'Lenic — What's for breakfast?

To my extended family: Jackie, Whitney, Wade and Wes Hantz and Mom Sharon Harrold for all the great holidays and summer vacations that helped me continue to hone my craft.

To Leyla, my beautiful daughter, who at age 10 had the foresight to convince me to begin collecting my recipes; something that eventually led me to this publication.

And to Hank my ever-loving sous chef who thoroughly enjoys every morsel I cook (that drops on the floor)!